CRAFTY GIFTS

MORE THAN 20 HANDMADE GIFTS TO GIVE

Project Editor Elizabeth Yeates
Designer Alison Gardner
Jacket Design Alison Gardner
Production Editor Heather Blagden
Producer Denitsa Kenanska
Special Sales Creative Project Manager
Alison Donovan

First published in Great Britain in 2015
by Dorling Kindersley Limited
DK, One Embassy Gardens, 8 Viaduct Gardens,
London, SW11 7BW

Material previously published in Craft (2012)

The authorised representative in the EEA
is Dorling Kindersley
Verlag GmbH. Arnulfstr. 124, 80636 Munich, Germany

A CIP catalogue record for this book is available from
the British Library.
ISBN 978-0-2414-5980-5

For the curious
www.dk.com

This book was made with
Forest Stewardship Council ™ certified paper –
one small step in DK's commitment to a sustainable future.
For more information go to **www.dk.com/our-green-pledge**

Contents

Introduction

WHETHER YOU ARE A BEGINNER OR A SEASONED CRAFTSPERSON, THERE IS ALWAYS SOMETHING NEW TO LEARN. THIS EXTENSIVE CRAFT COLLECTION PROVIDES A VALUABLE REFERENCE FOR A WIDE RANGE OF TECHNIQUES AND IT'S THE PERFECT WAY TO SAMPLE NEW CRAFTS. WHETHER YOU HAVE A PENCHANT FOR PAPER AND PAINT, FABRIC AND THREAD, CLAY, WAX, OR WIRE, THERE'LL BE SOMETHING IN THIS BOOK TO INSPIRE AND INSTRUCT YOU ON YOUR CRAFTING JOURNEY.

Crafting allows you to explore your creative side and it can be very addictive. Once you see how easy and satisfying it can be to make things yourself, you'll want to do it again and again. There is a wholesome satisfaction in making something from scratch, whether it's for yourself or for a loved one. The creative process can be just as fulfilling as the finished result – though it does help if the thing you have made is something to be proud of.

With this in mind, the techniques outlined in this book have been carefully written and illustrated in order to help build your skills and your confidence – and there is a dazzling array of inspirational projects, each broken down into manageable steps to help you produce perfect results.

To help you find the crafts to suit you, the book is divided into six chapters. With clear illustrations throughout and each project explained step-by-step, you'll be guided through every stage, so you can feel confident in attempting an unfamiliar craft and acquiring a new skill. Some techniques require particular equipment, so ensure you are able to source these tools before beginning.

None of the projects requires any particular expertise, most can be done without having to spend money on specialist tools or equipment, and all of them can be done at home using everyday resources. The projects have been devised by a team of talented and experienced craftspeople, and each project has been tried and tested to ensure a great outcome.

To make sure you get the best results, get organized. It's a good idea to read through your chosen project thoroughly before you begin, then make sure you gather all the tools and materials you will need. Some projects can be messy, so it's advisable not to wear your best clothes but to cover up with an old shirt or overalls. The same applies to your work surfaces: use old newspapers or plastic sheeting to cover the work table as certain concoctions – paints, dyes, and melted wax among others – might stain or damage surfaces they come into contact with.

Take your time, follow the instructions carefully, and before you know it you'll have created something to be proud of: something to grace your home, perhaps, something to wear, or something to give away as a present. Best of all is the enjoyment of making and the satisfaction of developing new skills or unearthing hidden talents. Embrace your creativity!

Textile crafts

Fabric marbling TECHNIQUES

Fabric marbling requires patience and can get messy, so always make sure your work surfaces are properly protected. You'll need to experiment with various tools and colours before you settle on a pattern you like.

Preparing the bath

Follow the manufacturer's instructions to make a marbling bath. Dissolve 1 teaspoon of "size" in 1 litre (1¾pt) cold water in a large plastic tub and stir well. For best results, leave to set overnight or for at least two hours before using.

Skimming the surface of the bath

As the bath has been left to settle, you'll need to break the tension on the surface. Do this by skimming the surface with newspaper scrunched into a ball. You'll also need to do this every time you apply fresh dyes.

Adding colour and creating patterns

1 Add a few drops of marbling dye on the surface of the bath so that it is completely covered with dye, then skim the surface with newspaper.

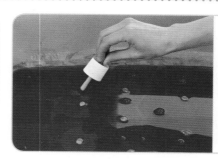

2 Add more drops of the first colour again to cover the surface, then dot a second colour onto the surface in a regular or random arrangement.

3 To create swirls, draw a marbling comb across the surface, from one edge of the tray to the other, pulling the dyes to create a wavy marbled effect.

4 Use a stylus, the end of a paintbrush, or other pointed implement to manipulate the colours and create individual swirls.

Experimenting with patterns

The bath solution improves the more you use it, so view your first few attempts as experiments. Always pre-wash the cotton fabric to make it more absorbent and practise with remnants of fabric, adding more dyes, skimming, and then printing to get an understanding of the patterns that can be created. Always wear rubber gloves to protect your hands from staining.

Marbling the fabric

1 Once you're happy with the marbled effect, lay the fabric onto the surface in one go, patting it gently to ensure there are no creases. Do not move the fabric as this will spoil the pattern.

2 Holding on to two corners, lift the fabric up swiftly, holding it over the tub to allow excess water and ink to drip off.

Fixing the colour

1 Leave the fabric to dry face up flat on a towel. Don't hang it up or wash it at this stage as the colours may run.

2 When the fabric is dry, it will be stiff due to the residue from the bath. Rinse under cold running water, then hang up to dry.

3 To fix the colour, iron the fabric on a medium setting. The fabric can now be washed.

Marbled napkins PROJECT

The unpredictability of marbling is what makes it such a fun craft. Each time you manipulate the dyes, new patterns emerge. If you don't like the pattern, simply skim off the dyes with newspaper and start again. If you like what you see, you can capture it on fabric forever. This introduction to fabric marbling shows you how to create a set of swirling marbled napkins.

YOU WILL NEED

- large shallow plastic tub
- measuring jug
- teaspoon
- marbling size
- newspaper
- blue and green marbling dyes
- marbling comb
- stylus or similar pointed implement
- rubber gloves
- 4 pre-washed white cotton napkins
- old towel
- iron

1 Make a marbling bath by dissolving 1 teaspoon of size in 1 litre (1¾pt) cold water in a tub. Leave to set overnight or for at least two hours. Skim the surface with a ball of newspaper to break the tension.

2 Dot a few drops of blue dye evenly across the surface of the bath. Skim the surface with newspaper before adding more blue dye. Then add a few drops of green dye in between the blue blocks of colour.

3 Draw a marbling comb across the surface of the bath, using a swift movement. If you want a more complex pattern, repeat the movement or use the stylus to create more swirls.

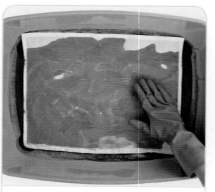

4 Wearing rubber gloves to protect your hands, carefully lower a napkin onto the surface of the bath. Pat it down gently then swiftly remove it. Repeat for the other napkins, skimming the bath and adding more dye each time.

5 Leave the napkins to dry face up flat on a towel, then rinse under cold running water. Hang up to dry, then iron on a medium setting to fix the dyes.

Fabric painting TECHNIQUES

Fabric paints are a permanent way to colour fabrics. They dry quite hard when applied but soften once the fabric has been washed. They can be mixed to create new shades or used straight from the pot, but it's best not to dilute them as you would water-based paints, as this reduces the pigmentation.

Preparing the fabric

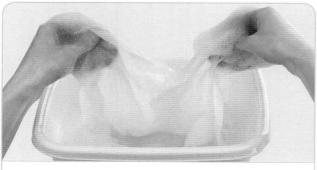

1 Always pre-wash the fabric to make it more absorbent. Rinse and hang up to dry.

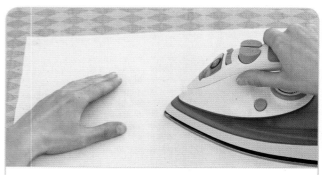

2 Once the fabric is dry, iron it to remove any creases. The surface of the fabric should be as smooth as possible, almost like a sheet of paper.

Transferring a template

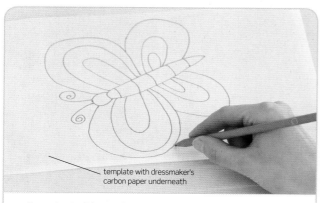

template with dressmaker's carbon paper underneath

1 Lay a sheet of dressmaker's carbon paper face down on the fabric and secure the template on top. Use a sharp pencil to trace over the template, then remove the carbon paper.

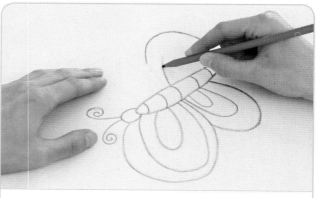

2 If the lines on the fabric are too faint, go over them again with a pencil.

Applying paint

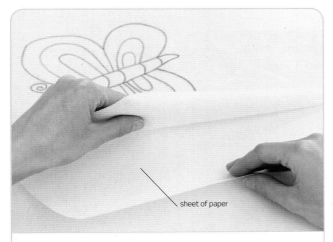

sheet of paper

1 If you're painting onto a double layer of fabric (such as a bag for instance), place a sheet of paper inside the bag to prevent the paint seeping through to the layer underneath.

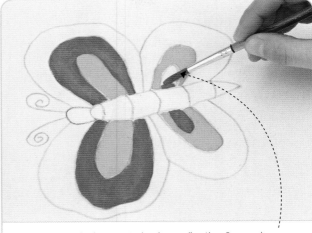

2 Apply the paint in even strokes in one direction. Some colours, especially lighter colours, may require more than one coat. Allow each coat to dry before applying a second.

3 Once the main design is complete and dry, add details with a fine paintbrush or draw on outlines with a fabric paint pen.

Fixing the colour

Leave the paint to dry for 24 hours. Place the fabric face down and iron on a high setting to fix the colours. The fabric can now be washed.

13

Shoe bag PROJECT

Shoe bags are great for when you're travelling or if you like to store your footwear away neatly. Customize a plain bag by painting on a shoe-themed motif, or draw designs that look like your own shoes, making them easy to identify. Use a mix of fabric paint and fabric paint pens – you can be as intricate as you like or stick to designing with block colours.

YOU WILL NEED

For the drawstring bag

- 1m x 69cm (40 x 27in) pre-washed white cotton
- cutting shears
- dressmaking pins
- sewing machine
- white thread
- 150cm (60in) ribbon
- iron

For the motif

- dressmaker's carbon paper
- pencil
- sheet of paper
- fabric paints
- paintbrushes
- fabric paint pen

1 To make the bag, fold the fabric over by 5cm (2in) along one long side. Pin and tack. Using a straight stitch on the sewing machine, sew along the edge of the fold to create the ribbon casing.

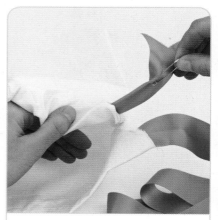

2 Fold the fabric in half lengthways with the casing on the outside. Sew the bottom and side edges using a straight stitch, stopping at the casing using a safety pin. Feed the ribbon through the casing then turn the bag to the right side.

3 Transfer the template on p.120 onto one side of the bag, following **transferring a template** on p.12. Make sure the design is centred.

4 Slip a sheet of paper inside the bag to protect the bottom layer. To prevent the colours merging, allow each colour to dry before painting the next. Add a second coat of paint if required.

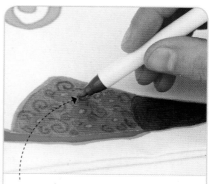

5 Use the fabric paint pen to outline the shoe and draw on the swirls. Leave to dry for 24 hours.

6 Place the bag face down and iron on a high setting to fix the colours.

Batik TECHNIQUES

Batik is the art of painting fabric using a wax resist. Apply the wax using a paintbrush or tjanting, then paint over the fabric – the waxed areas will repel the paint and retain their base colour. You can use this technique to build up multiple layers of colour and to produce fabulous "crackle" effects. This technique can also be done using a wax pot and hot wax.

Stretching the fabric

Using three-pronged pins, pin all four corners of the fabric to a frame, ensuring the fabric is straight and taut. Next, pin halfway along each side, then pin at regular intervals so that there is a pin every 5 to 7.5cm (2 to 3in).

2 Using a fine paintbrush, paint cold wax over the traced lines: these lines will remain white on the finished piece. Leave to dry naturally for about 20 minutes, or for speed, use a hairdryer on a cool setting.

tjanting

5 To add further detail, paint a line of cold wax around the inside of the petals. These lines will act as a barrier, keeping the next colour confined to the edges of the petals. Here a tjanting has been used, but you could also use a fine paintbrush.

Painting the design

1 Fix the template under the fabric and trace the design onto the fabric using a vanishing fabric marker pen.

3 Use a medium paintbrush to paint the flower centre and petals with iron-fixed silk paint, right up to the wax lines. Allow the paint to dry.

4 Paint the background using a sponge brush dipped in paint. Paint up to the edges of the flower but not over it. Allow to dry.

6 Once the wax has dried, paint between the two wax lines in the petal colour. The second coat will give a darker colour.

Adding crackle

1 Dip a small sponge into cold wax and brush it over the entire surface of the piece. Leave to dry for 20 minutes.

2 Remove the fabric from the frame and scrunch it to crackle the wax. The more you crumple the fabric, the more pronounced the crackle effect will be.

3 Spread the fabric out, face up, on a surface protected with plastic sheeting. Leaving some creases in place, paint over the background using a sponge brush.

4 Wait a few seconds for the colour to sink into the fabric. Darker lines showing on the reverse of the fabric indicate that the crackle effect is working. When you are satisfied with the effect, you can halt the process using a hairdryer on a cool setting.

Setting the paint

Once the fabric is dry, sandwich it between layers of newspaper and iron for three minutes per 30cm (12in) square, keeping the iron moving. This will set the paints and absorb some of the wax. Repeat with clean newspaper until most of the wax has been absorbed.

Removing residual dye and wax

1 Rinse the fabric in cold water to remove the residual dye and more of the wax. Stir 1 tablespoon of Wax-Out liquid into 2 litres (3½pts) warm (30 to 40°C/ 86 to 104°F) water. Soak the fabric for 10 minutes, stirring gently (or follow the manufacturer's instructions) to remove the remaining wax.

2 Remove the fabric from the Wax-Out solution and wash it gently in hot water with a little detergent. Iron on the reverse while damp.

Cushion cover PROJECT

Batik is a fun way to make a beautiful cushion cover. This project makes one cushion cover with an organic branch and leaf design. Start with plain white cotton and use wax and paints to build up the design in layers. You may wish to paint the back of the cushion to match the front before sewing the back and front together. Make the cover in an envelope-style, or stitch on a zip or buttons.

YOU WILL NEED

- 2 x 45cm (18in) squares of white 100% cotton fabric
- scissors
- 45cm (18in) square wooden frame
- three-pronged pins
- vanishing fabric marker pen
- fine and medium paintbrushes
- cold batik wax
- iron-fixed silk paints in yellow, light green, and dark green
- palette
- water pot
- sponge brush

- plastic sheeting
- small sponge
- Wax-Out liquid
- newspaper
- iron
- detergent

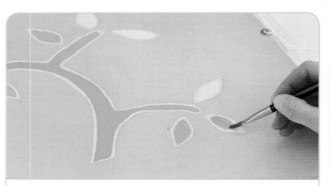

1 Stretch and pin one square of fabric to the frame. Using the vanishing fabric marker pen, trace the outline of the template on p.121 on the centre of the fabric. With a fine paintbrush, paint cold wax over the traced lines. Leave to dry for about 20 minutes. Paint the background yellow using a sponge brush, then paint the branch and leaves using light green paint. Leave to dry for 20 minutes.

2 With the template as a guide, paint the lines on the branch and the veins on the leaves. Use cold wax and a fine paintbrush. Leave to dry for 20 minutes.

3 Using the dark green, paint alternate stripes on the branch and on half of each leaf. Leave to dry for 20 minutes.

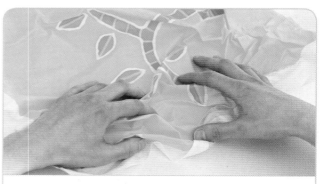

4 Dip a small sponge in cold wax and brush it over the entire piece so that it is covered in a layer of wax. Leave to dry for 20 minutes. Remove the fabric from the frame and scrunch it to crackle the wax. Protect the work surface with plastic sheeting then spread the fabric out, face up. Paint over the yellow background in the dark green, using a sponge brush. Wait a few seconds for the colour to sink into the fabric. When you are satisfied with the effect, use a hairdryer on a cool setting to halt the process.

5 Once the fabric is dry, follow **setting the paint** on p17. Then rinse the fabric in cold water to remove all traces of dye before soaking in a solution of Wax-Out liquid for 10 minutes. Wash gently in hot soapy water then iron on the reverse while damp. If you wish, you can paint the second square of fabric (the back of the cushion cover) in yellow, then add crackle by using a layer of cold wax and the dark green paint.

Patchwork TECHNIQUES

The secret to successful patchwork is accurate cutting then matching seams carefully before stitching them together. If the seams don't quite match up, try stretching the shorter edge slightly before sewing to ensure accuracy. One of the most important tools for patchwork is an iron; use it on the steam setting when pressing cotton to keep the seams flat and crisp.

Cutting patchwork fabric

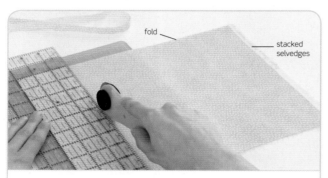

fold
stacked selvedges

1 Fold a piece of fabric selvedge to selvedge. Press with a steam iron, then place the folded fabric on a cutting mat. Trim the left edge straight, then align a patchwork ruler on the fold so that its right edge is 8cm (3¹/₄in) from the trimmed edge. Cut along the ruler to make a strip. Move the ruler along to cut more strips the same width.

trimmed fold

2 Turn the double-layer strip and cut along the fold to make two strips. Using the lines on the ruler as a guide, cut the strips into 8cm (3¹/₄in) squares. If you don't have a rotary cutter, draw pencil lines to mark squares and cut along the lines with dressmaking shears.

Sewing patchwork pieces

Place two squares with right sides together under the presser foot. Line up the edge of the fabric with the presser foot. Adjust the needle position if necessary to make the seam allowance exactly 6mm (¹/₄in). Stitch the seam. For speed, you can stitch a row of squares one after the other, leaving a small thread gap between them.

Making a complete row

Cut the pairs of squares apart, then stitch one end of a pair to the end of another pair. Repeat to make a complete row, then press all seam allowances in the same direction. Press seams in alternate rows the opposite way to reduce bulk when sewing rows together.

Joining rows

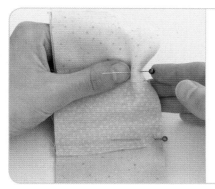

1 Place two rows of squares right sides together. To reduce bulk, ensure the seam allowances in each row face in the opposite directions. Pin together using glass-headed pins and match the seams exactly.

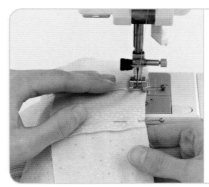

2 Using the edge of the presser foot as a guide, stitch the two rows together, stitching over each pin carefully as you go. Stitch all the rows together then remove the pins. Press all the horizontal seams towards the bottom of the patchwork.

Adding a border

1 Cut two strips the width of the patchwork and twice the depth of the border, plus 12mm (1/2in). With wrong sides together, press in half lengthways and press one long edge over by 6mm (1/4in). With right sides together, pin then stitch the unpressed edge to the top of the patchwork. Repeat on the bottom, then press seams outwards.

6mm (1/4in) turn-over

2 For the long sides, cut two strips the length of the patchwork, plus the top and bottom borders. Press and stitch as in Step 1. Begin stitching 6mm (1/4in) from the edge and finish 6mm (1/4in) from the bottom. Repeat on the other side, then press seams outwards.

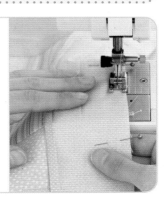

Adding wadding

1 Cut the wadding and backing fabric to fit exactly between the pressed fold lines in the middle of the border strips. Lay wadding then backing fabric face up on the reverse side of the patchwork.

2 Fold the border along the fold lines at the top and bottom, and pin. Fold the sides to make neat corners. Slip stitch the border to the backing fabric.

Joining the layers

Using strands of embroidery cotton, backstitch through all layers at regular intervals at the intersections. To finish, tie a reef (square) knot at each stitch and trim neatly.

Patchwork bedspread PROJECT

Patchwork is a craft suitable for anyone who can use a sewing machine. This project is ideal if you are new to sewing by machine as all the seams are straight. If you can't find the exact fabrics used here, or wish to change the colour scheme, look for alternative fabrics with the same intensity of colour to achieve a similar overall look.

YOU WILL NEED

- 225cm (2½yd) olive green fabric (115cm/45in) wide
- 175cm (2yd) tiny blue spot fabric (115cm/45in) wide
- 75cm (30in) each of white polka dot fabric and wheel pattern fabric (115cm/45in) wide
- cutting mat
- patchwork ruler
- rotary cutter or dressmaking shears
- sewing machine
- cotton thread in matching colours
- iron
- glass-headed pins
- 145cm x 2m (57 x 79in) thin (2oz) polyester wadding
- 145cm x 2m (57 x 79in) backing fabric
- needle

1 Cut twelve 16cm (6¼in) squares of olive green fabric, 59 squares of tiny blue spot fabric, 22 squares of white polka dot fabric, and 24 squares of wheel pattern fabric.

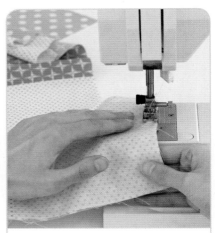

2 Arrange the squares as shown on the diagram on p.124. Following **sewing patchwork pieces** and **making a complete row** on p.20, stitch the squares together in rows.

3 Press the seam allowances on each row to one side. Following the diagram, press the seam allowances on alternate rows in the opposite direction.

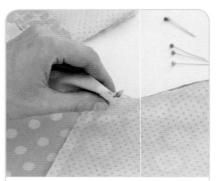

4 Pin then stitch the first two rows together, following **joining rows** on p.21. Repeat for the other rows. Press all the horizontal seams towards the bottom of the patchwork.

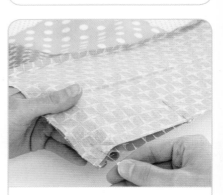

5 Following Step 1 of **adding a border** on p.21, stitch 15cm (6in) wide strips of olive green fabric to the top and bottom of the patchwork panel. Follow Step 2 to attach borders to the sides, then press.

6 Press the whole panel. With the patchwork face down, lay the wadding and backing fabric, face up, on top. Fold the border edges and corners over neatly and slip stitch. Following **joining the layers** on p.21, stitch ties through the layers at regular intervals.

Appliqué TECHNIQUES

Appliqué involves applying fabric shapes to a base fabric and stitching around the shapes. It's a great way of using small pieces of your favourite fabrics to embellish any fabric item. The simplest way to appliqué requires a product called bonding web, which is a thin web of dry glue with a paper backing. Bonding web allows you to create iron-on appliqué shapes very easily. If you are new to appliqué, keep the shapes simple at first before moving on to more complicated creations.

Creating the appliqué

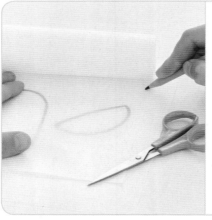

1 Choose the image you want to use for your appliqué and select your fabrics. For this example, we are using a simple hand-drawn owl shape with separate wings. Cut out a piece of bonding web big enough for the owl's body and wings.

2 Place the bonding web over the body and the wings so that the glue side of the bonding web is facing down and the paper side is uppermost. Trace over the images using a pencil.

3 With the iron on a medium setting, iron the pieces of bonding web, glue-side down, onto the reverse of your chosen fabrics. If your fabric has a directional pattern, make sure that the pieces are positioned so that the pattern will be the right way up on the finished shape.

4 Cut out the fabric shapes, paying particular attention around the curves to make sure they are smooth.

24

Applying the appliqué

1 Peel the backing paper of the bonding web off the owl shape, making sure that the adhesive, now on the fabric, does not stick to itself.

2 Position the body of the owl onto the fabric you are attaching it to and iron it in position.

3 Sew around the shape by hand or with a sewing machine. You can use either a straight stitch or zigzag stitch to do this. If you are using a straight stitch, as shown here, keep your stitching 2 to 3 mm (1/10 to 1/8in) in from the edge of the shape.

4 Position and iron the wings in place and sew around them, as explained in Step 3.

Decorating the appliqué

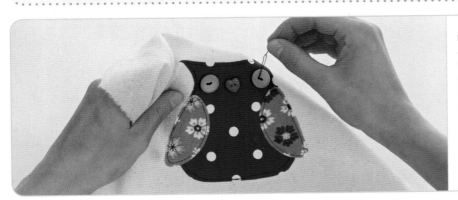

Embellishments such as buttons, sequins, and beads can be sewn on to add interest. Sew on two round buttons for the eyes using contrasting thread. Sew on an orange heart-shaped button for the beak using matching thread.

Appliqué throw PROJECT

A mixture of patterned and plain fabrics has been used to adorn this soft cream-coloured lambswool throw. Of course, you don't have to use the same fabrics that are used here, but when choosing your fabrics, spend time selecting ones that work well together. We have added an assortment of buttons to the flower centres to give the throw a charming homespun look.

YOU WILL NEED

- 4.5m x 50cm (5yd x 20in) bonding web
- pencil
- scissors
- 60 x 150cm (23 x 60in) each of plain light green linen fabric, grey/green floral cotton fabric, and pink floral cotton fabric
- 50 x 70cm (20 x 27½in) each of pale pink cotton fabric and green polka dot fabric
- iron
- 140 x 190cm (55 x 75in) plain cream woollen or fleece throw
- pins
- sewing machine
- cream, olive green, dark grey, and pink sewing threads
- 30 assorted medium-size buttons in grey, cream, red, and green
- sewing needle

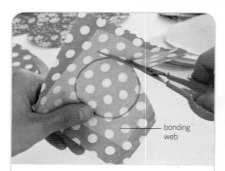

bonding web

1 Using the templates on pp.122-3, prepare 15 plain light green base circles, 15 smaller flowers in grey/green floral, 15 outer circles for them in pale pink, and 15 smaller inner circles for them in green polka dot. Then prepare 15 larger flowers in pink floral, 15 outer circles for them in green polka dot, and 15 smaller inner circles for them in pale pink.

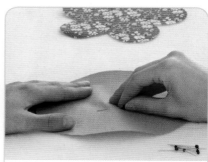

2 Peel away the backing paper of the bonding web and arrange a row of five alternating green circles and pink floral print flowers across the top of the throw, starting with a green circle. Pin them in position. Then arrange the second row, starting with a pink floral print flower. Iron them in position. Repeat these two rows twice more.

3 Sew around the edges of the green circles and pink floral print flowers in straight stitch. Peel away the backing paper on the grey/green flowers and iron them onto the green circles then stitch around these. When sewing the appliqués, keep cream thread in the bobbin and match the top threads to your fabrics.

4 Apply the two centre circles to each flower. Stitch around the pink circles in pink sewing thread and the green polka dot circles in olive green thread, remembering to keep cream thread in the bobbin throughout.

5 To finish, sew a button to each of the flower centres.

Papercraft gifts

Papermaking TECHNIQUES

Paper has come a long way since the ancient Chinese first made paper in the second century BC. The Egyptians used papyrus, our ancestors used animal skins, but we gradually developed a process of making an even surface to write or draw on from pulped fibres. To make your own paper, use paper such as printer paper that's already been pulped once.

Making a mould and deckle

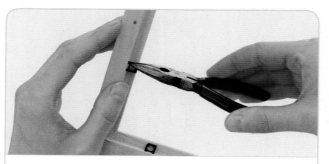

1 You will need two sturdy picture frames of roughly the same size to make a mould and deckle. If one is slightly larger, it should be the mould. Remove any hooks, clips, or wires from the frames.

2 To make the mould, stretch netting or fine mesh (plastic mosquito mesh works well) tightly across the flat side of the frame and staple all around the edge. This side is the top of the mould.

3 Hold the mould so that the netting is uppermost. Place the deckle flat side down on top of the mould. The deckle "frames" the paper pulp, forming a neat edge all round.

Selecting paper to use

Some papers work better than others for papermaking. Suitable papers include bank statements, printer paper, old letters, and other non-glossy papers without too much dark printing. Papers that aren't suitable are glossy papers, such as magazines and colour supplements, or recycled paper, such as newspapers and kitchen paper, whose fibres are too short. Try to stick to one dominant colour.

Shredding and soaking paper

Shred the paper into short 1cm (³⁄₈in) wide strips. Soak in a tub of water for at least a couple of hours – overnight is better – to allow the water to penetrate the fibres.

Building a couching mound

1 Lay some open newspapers on your work surface. Build a pile of newspapers, one folded over the next, concertina-style, about 5 to 8cm (2 to 3in) high and a little wider and longer than the mould. There should be no dip in the centre or water will pool there.

2 Drape several old towels over the mound of newspapers and roll them up around the edges. This is the "couching mound", on which you'll lay your sheets of paper to drain.

Making paper pulp

1 Half-fill a large shallow tray with cold water. Scoop some of the soaked paper into a food processor, cover with water, and blitz until it resembles a paste. Empty the paste into the tray. Repeat until the water in the tray is like a thickish soup.

Angelina fibres

2 If you're planning to add other fibres, glitter, or Angelina, stir them in now. Yarn and/or flower petals can also be added to the mix, or you can add them later if you want to control what their final position will be. Stir the mixture thoroughly.

Making paper from pulp

1 Hold the mould and deckle together, with the deckle flat side down, on top. Slide them into the tray of pulp at a 45° angle. Scoop up some of the pulp. Carefully withdraw the mould and deckle, shaking gently as you do so. This will help distribute the pulp evenly, which avoids holes in the paper.

2 Let the water drain through the netting, then tilt the mould and deckle gently towards one corner to allow the excess water to run off.

3 Lift off the deckle, then carefully lay an absorbent cloth over the pulp.

4 Align the edge of the mould with the edge of the couching mound. Quickly flip the mould containing the pulp on top of the mound.

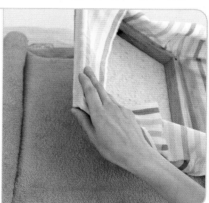

5 Run your fingers over the netting: the pulp will start to come away from the mould and stick to the cloth beneath.

6 Carefully peel away the mould. Start by lifting one corner or side: the pulp should remain on the cloth. Run your hand over any obstinate areas to help release the pulp from the net. Leave the pulp to drain.

Draining and drying the paper

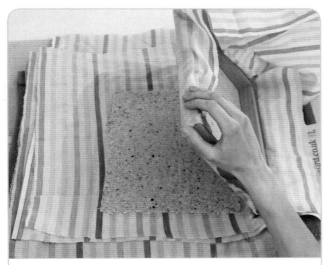

heavy weight

1 Cover the sheet of paper with cloth and start work on the next sheet. Build up a pile of cloths and sheets, one on top of the other, on the couching mound. When the "pulp soup" gets thin, blitz some more soaked paper and add it to the pulp mix.

2 Once you've used up as much of the pulp as you can and before the sheets of paper get too thin, lay one final cloth and a newspaper or towel over the top of the mound. Then lay a chopping board on top, pile some weights onto it, and leave for 10 minutes to squeeze any remaining water out of the sheets.

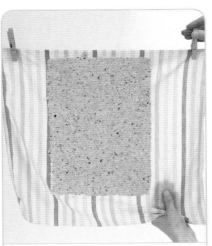

3 Remove the weights and chopping board and carefully peel off the top cloth.

4 The sheet of paper usually adheres to the cloth beneath it. Peg it onto a line or drying rack to dry. Lift and peg each successive cloth with paper attached. Leave to dry overnight or for a few days if the weather is damp.

5 When the paper is dry, remove it from the cloth. If it doesn't come away easily, iron it with the cloth face upwards, then peel the cloth off. If the paper has curled at the edges, press it flat with a medium-hot iron.

Petal writing paper PROJECT

Make some unique and decorative paper to write a special letter to a friend or to mount a precious picture on. Handmade paper is easy to make but hard to beat when it comes to making an impression. Use paper that you would otherwise recycle and add dried petals and scraps of coloured or metallic thread to create a really special effect.

YOU WILL NEED

- paper to shred (see p.30)
- shredder
- tub
- food processor
- large shallow tray
- red or pink food colouring (optional)
- newspaper
- old towels
- mould and deckle
- dried flower petals
- short scraps of coloured thread (optional)
- absorbent cloths a little larger than the mould
- chopping board
- heavy weight
- iron

1 Shred and soak the paper. Make the pulp following **making paper pulp** on p.31. If the pulp looks greyish, stir in a little red or pink food colouring. Follow **building a couching mound** on p.31.

2 Slide the mould and deckle into the tray and scoop up some pulp. Shake to distribute the pulp evenly, then tilt the mould and deckle to allow excess water to run off.

3 Scatter dried petals around the edge of the paper so they won't obscure any writing. You may wish to scatter a little more pulp over the petals, or lay some scraps of thread over them to "fix" them to the paper.

4 Lift the deckle then carefully place an absorbent cloth over the paper, taking care not to disturb the petals.

5 Flip the cloth and mould over onto the couching mound to drain. Run your fingers over the netting to dislodge the sheet of paper, then gently lift the mould off. Place absorbent cloth over the sheet of paper.

6 Continue making sheets until the pulp gets too thin, then drain the paper using a heavy weight on a chopping board to help squeeze out the water. Hang up to dry. When dry, iron the reverse side of the sheets, so as not to scorch or disturb the petals.

Papier-mâché TECHNIQUES

The term papier-mâché is French for "chewed paper", and describes a variety of techniques where paper is saturated with paste and moulded into a shape which, when dry, forms a hard, durable shell. It is remarkable what a magical transformation can be achieved with old newspapers and paste, which makes papier-mâché a great recycling craft, ideal for creating decorative objects for the home such as vases, bowls, boxes, pencil pots, plaques, and trays.

Making a base

1 Select suitable plastic or cardboard containers that can be joined together to create interesting, one-off shapes.

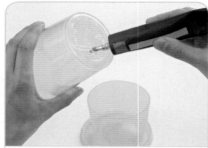

2 Use an all-purpose glue to join the components together.

3 Use plastic bags, rolled into sausages or crumpled up, to pad out the basic form. Stick these in place with sticky tape.

Preparing the papier-mâché

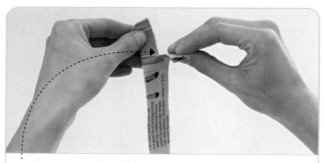

1 The paper should be absorbent: use old newspapers or pages torn from telephone directories. Tear the paper into manageable strips – don't cut it; the torn edges, when overlapped, will form a smooth surface without too many ridges.

2 Mix wallpaper paste in a bowl, following the instructions on the packet. Most pastes contain fungicides, so if you have sensitive skin, you may wish to wear rubber gloves. Protect your work surface with newspaper or plastic sheeting.

Building layers

1 It's important to ensure that each paper strip is saturated with wallpaper paste. Dip it into the paste and use your fingers to remove surplus paste.

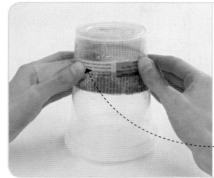

2 Apply the paper strip to the object and smooth it out with your fingertips, expelling air bubbles. Make sure you cover not only the surfaces but also all the edges and joins.

3 Build up lots of layers – at least eight or nine – to ensure a successful result.

4 Newsprint creates a neutral grey surface but if you wish to cover this up, apply a few layers of tissue paper; this will help to disguise the print and also creates a smoother surface.

tissue paper

Decorating the object

1 Allow the papier-mâché to dry completely before decorating. If there are any ridges or bumps, lightly sand the surface using fine sandpaper.

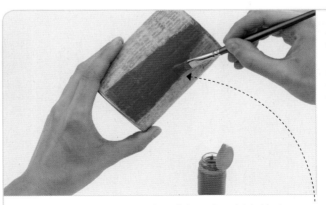

2 If you wish to decorate the surface of the papier-mâché object, you can paint it with water-based paints such as poster paints, watercolours, gouache, acrylics, or even household emulsion. Apply an (optional) undercoat of white paint if you want to use very light colours.

3 Once you have decorated the item, finish by sealing it with several coats of water-based varnish.

Papier-mâché bowl PROJECT

This decorative bowl is made from a disposable plastic receptacle – the kind sold in supermarkets containing salads – and the cardboard plinth from the centre of a ball of knitting yarn, plus a couple of plastic bags to pad out the rim. You can create a stylish bowl from these humble components, and decorate the surface using coloured tissue paper and a smattering of metal leaf.

YOU WILL NEED

- plastic bowl
- cardboard cylinder
- all-purpose glue
- 1–2 plastic bags
- sticky tape
- card
- scissors
- wallpaper paste
- newspaper, torn into strips
- PVA glue
- medium and large soft paintbrushes
- coloured tissue papers
- metal leaf size
- metal leaf
- water-based varnish

1 Glue the cardboard cylinder to the base of the bowl. Roll up one or two plastic bags and tape them under the rim of the bowl. Cut a circle of card to fit the base of the cylinder and glue or tape it in place.

2 Mix up wallpaper paste. Dip strips of newspaper in the paste, squeeze off excess paste with your fingers, and apply the saturated strips to the inside and outside of the bowl and all over the plinth, smoothing out each strip as you go.

3 Continue in this way until the whole piece is covered, then repeat until you have built up at least eight or nine layers. Leave to dry completely (this can take several days or even weeks, depending on temperature and humidity).

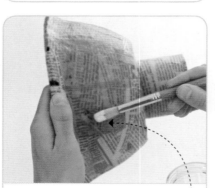

4 Once dry, brush the surface of the entire piece with PVA diluted with water to the consistency of single cream, then apply pieces of coloured tissue paper, brushing each one with diluted PVA. Apply two or three layers of tissue, then leave to dry.

5 Cut out circles from tissue paper in a contrasting colour, and glue these in place, using more of the diluted PVA. Leave to dry for several hours or overnight.

6 Once the tissue layers are dry, paint the rim with metal leaf size. Leave for 10 minutes, then apply metal leaf over the size, rubbing down gently with clean fingers. Use a large, soft brush to brush away any excess. Protect with two or three coats of varnish.

Découpage TECHNIQUES

Découpage is the craft of decorating an object with paper cutouts glued in place. If you take the time to apply many coats of varnish over the paper cutouts, they will appear to sink into the surface and will look as though they are part of the object and not merely stuck on. Choose from the wide range of printed papers available: gift wrap, magazine pages, catalogues, and brochures – and even papers with repeat motifs printed specifically for découpage.

Choosing your materials

Look for papers that have printed motifs that are separate and do not overlap with other parts of the design. This will provide you with individual elements to cut out. Make sure you have enough of your chosen motifs: buy two or more sheets of paper, if necessary.

Cutting out the motifs

1 Rough-cut the paper: this means cutting out each motif roughly, leaving a border of paper all round.

2 Using small scissors with pointed blades to ensure accuracy, cut out each motif very carefully. For best results, keep the scissors quite static and move the paper, rather than the other way round.

3 Make sure you cut away any areas of background within the motif. This is particularly important if, say, the background is white and the object you are sticking the motif onto is coloured.

Arranging and glueing the cutouts

1 Try out your design before sticking anything down. Move the cutouts around until you are happy with the arrangement.

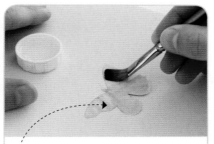

2 Brush découpage medium or PVA glue diluted with water to the consistency of thin cream onto the back of each cutout. Make sure each piece is thoroughly covered and there are no dry areas.

3 Place the glued cutouts in place and smooth out the paper, expelling any air bubbles. Use the same brush you used to apply the medium to the back of the cutouts.

Varnishing the piece

When the cutout is stuck down, leave it to dry, then apply a coat of clear varnish. You can choose a matt or gloss varnish, depending on the effect you want to achieve. Apply several coats of varnish, allowing each one to dry before applying the next.

Adding embellishments

1 To highlight small areas of the design, stick on flat-backed gems, which will add texture and sparkle.

2 Glitter also adds a touch of sparkle to a finished design. Simply apply dabs of glue using a cocktail stick to the areas you wish to highlight.

glitter

3 Then sprinkle on glitter, tip off any excess, and leave to dry thoroughly.

Keepsake box PROJECT

You can use découpage to decorate a number of different objects. A plain cardboard box is an ideal candidate for this technique. Choose one that is sturdy and well-proportioned, and look for printed papers with attractive flower heads and leaves – such as these pansies – to combine into an elegant floral arrangement to decorate the lid and sides of the box.

YOU WILL NEED
- printed papers
- small scissors with pointed blades
- cardboard box with lid
- soft paintbrush
- découpage medium or PVA glue diluted with water to the consistency of thin cream
- water-based gloss varnish

1 Cut out motifs roughly from printed paper then, using small scissors, cut out each one neatly, including areas between the leaves, stems, and petals.

2 Arrange the cutouts on the box until you are satisfied with the design. Take time to assess whether you have enough cutouts or whether you need to make more.

back of cutout

3 Using a soft paintbrush, apply découpage medium or diluted PVA glue all over the back of the cutout that will form the basis of your arrangement.

4 Place the pasted cutout in position on the box lid and smooth out, using the brush still loaded with medium. Repeat to complete the arrangement with the remaining cutouts.

5 Apply cutouts to the sides of the box in a similar way, avoiding the upper part which will be covered by the sides of the lid.

6 To protect the paper cutouts and to create an attractive finish, brush the box with several coats of varnish – ideally about six or more coats – leaving each coat to dry thoroughly before applying the next.

Quilling TECHNIQUES

Quilling, sometimes called paper filigree, is the centuries-old art of creating decorative shapes from narrow strips of paper. Various shapes can be formed, usually by first rolling the strips into tight coils, then allowing them to unroll slightly and pinching them. These can then be combined to make patterns, using the various shapes and colours to good effect. No special tools are needed – you can roll the strips around a cocktail stick – though quilling tools and pre-cut paper strips are readily available from craft suppliers.

Cutting paper strips

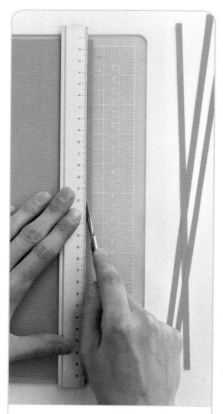

Use a metal ruler and craft knife over a cutting mat to cut narrow strips from a sheet of coloured paper. Strips can be any width, though 3mm (⅛in) is the most popular size.

Basic quilling

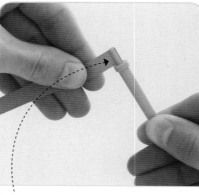

1 Insert one end of a paper strip into the slit in the quilling tool (or wrap the end around a cocktail stick).

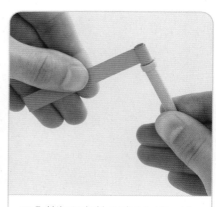

2 Twirl the tool with one hand while guiding the paper strip with the other, to wind the paper into a tight coil.

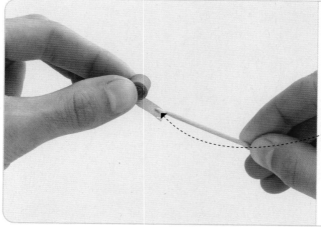

3 Slip the paper coil off the tool. If you want to use the quilled strip as a tight coil, use a cocktail stick to dab a spot of PVA glue to the end of the strip and stick in place.

Creating shapes

1 Allow the coiled paper to relax slightly to make a round coil that is more open in appearance, then glue the end in place.

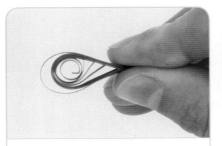

2 To create a teardrop shape – useful for flower petals and leaves – allow the coiled paper to unwind slightly before glueing the end in place, then pinch the coil in one place between finger and thumb.

3 To create a shape reminiscent of an eye – known as a marquise – allow the coiled paper to relax slightly, glue the end, then pinch the coil in two places, as shown.

4 For a triangular shape, pinch a coil that has relaxed slightly in three places. This shape is useful for flower motifs and leaves.

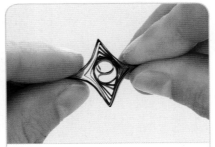

5 A relaxed coil pinched in four places is known as a star.

6 Create this heart shape by rolling a paper strip from both ends, then crease the centre of the strip so that the coils face each other.

Glueing and arranging

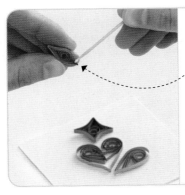

1 Use small dabs of PVA glue – which becomes transparent once dry – to glue shapes to a background.

2 Combine various shapes to make motifs that can be used to decorate greetings cards, labels, pictures, and book covers.

Quilled paper picture PROJECT

You will need only the most basic materials – strips of coloured paper, a quilling tool or cocktail stick, a piece of backing card, and glue – to create a decorative quilled picture. To display your work of art, choose a fairly deep frame, or mount the picture using a deep mount that accommodates the thickness of the paper strips and prevents them from touching the glass.

YOU WILL NEED

- 3mm (⅛in) wide paper strips in blue, yellow, red, green, and pale green
- quilling tool
- PVA glue
- cocktail sticks
- 25 x 20cm (10 x 8in) backing card

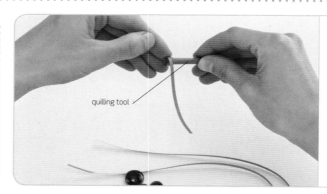

quilling tool

1 Make 15 coils in blue: make three tight coils, eight a little more relaxed, and four more relaxed still. Glue the ends in place.

2 Make three tight coils in yellow, then make seven teardrop shapes in red for the petals, glueing the ends in place.

3 Make six leaves using green paper strips and glue the ends.

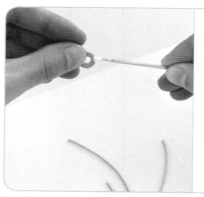

4 Fold pale green strips in half lengthways to create stems. Apply glue sparingly along the edges of the paper and place on the backing card, using the final image as a guide. Glue one yellow coil to form a flower centre.

5 Arrange the other quilled shapes in position. When you are happy with the arrangement, glue each shape in place.

Card-making TECHNIQUES

Homemade greetings cards are fun to make and show the recipient that you really care. Traditionally sent on special occasions such as birthdays and Christmas, they can also be sent to convey all kinds of messages – such as "thank you" and "good luck", or to convey various sentiments. Best of all, making your own cards requires only the most basic materials and this craft really allows you to express your creativity in a unique and individual way.

Making basic cards

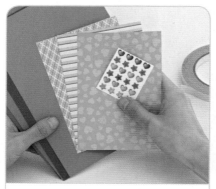

1 There is a wide range of card available to buy, both plain and patterned. For card-making, choose card stock that is sturdy but not too thick.

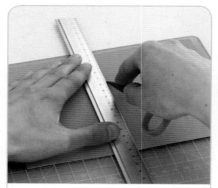

2 A rectangle of card folded in half makes a basic, single-fold card. To make folding easier and neater, score the centre line using the back blade of a pair of scissors and a metal ruler.

3 Cut a piece of paper to the same dimensions as the card or slightly smaller, and fold it in half, for an inner leaf on which to write your message. Punch two holes through both layers, on the centrefold.

4 Thread the ends of a length of ribbon through the holes of both layers and tie with a bow.

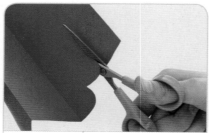

5 Additional folds create further design possibilities: a two-fold card gives six surfaces for decoration (three on the front and three on the back). Cut the corners in an interesting shape to add another dimension.

6 This scalloped edge creates an attractive effect. It can be left plain or decorated with stickers.

Making pop-ups

1 Pop-ups add an extra dimension to a single-fold card. Cut two slits at right angles to the folded edge, then score between the ends of these slits, parallel to the edge of the card, to create a rectangular "flap".

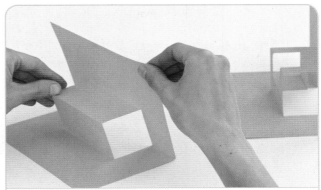

2 Fold across the scored lines to create the pop-up. By cutting and scoring a second set of lines, you can create another level of pop-up. Experiment on scrap paper first to make sure both sets of scored lines work together correctly.

Adding extra decorative elements

1 Combine shapes cut from plain and patterned card scraps to make components to decorate your card.

deckle-edged scissors

2 Use fancy scissors to cut decorative edges. Deckle-edged scissors are available from most craft suppliers, with a wide selection of different blades.

3 To add texture and interest, use small pieces cut from thick card, or use dimensional sticky pads to raise components off the surface of the card, creating a 3D effect.

Pop-up cake card PROJECT

Suitable for a number of different occasions, such as a greetings card or an invitation for a birthday, anniversary, or wedding perhaps – this pop-up card is impressive but uses the simplest techniques to maximum effect. All you need are some colourful card scraps, a steady hand, and a sharp craft knife. Vary the colour scheme to suit your own tastes and the occasion.

YOU WILL NEED

- 2 plain coloured pieces of card measuring 24 x 17cm (9¾ x 6¾in)
- metal ruler
- scissors
- pencil
- cutting mat
- craft knife
- printed and white card scraps
- deckle-edged scissors
- double-sided sticky tape
- hole punch
- narrow ribbon
- stickers
- glue stick

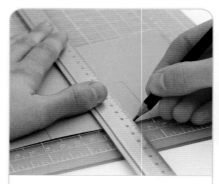

1 Score across the centre of one of the cards and fold in half. Measure 5cm (2in) in from each side and make two 5.5cm (2¼in) cuts at right angles to the folded edge at each of the marked points. Measure 1.5cm (⅝in) in from the cut lines and make two more 3.5cm (1⅜in) cuts.

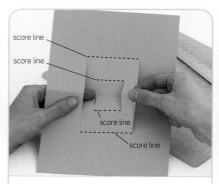

score line
score line
score line
score line

2 Score between the ends of the two pairs of parallel cuts. Open out the card, folding the larger pop-out inwards and the smaller, inner one outwards, as shown.

3 Using striped card, cut a rectangle 10 x 5.75cm (4 x 2½in) for the bottom tier. For the top tier, cut a piece 7 x 4.5cm (2¾ x 1¾in) then cut away strips to form candles. For the middle tier, cut a piece 8 x 4.5cm (3¼ x 1¾in) and cut away corners to create a tab to slot into the middle of the inner pop-up.

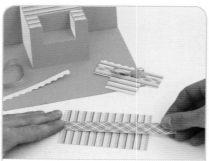

4 From the striped card, cut a piece to cover the top of the pop-up. From contrasting card, cut strips to fit across the tiers. Using deckle-edged scissors, cut strips of white card for borders. Punch pairs of holes in the centres of the card strips, insert short lengths of ribbon, and tie in bows.

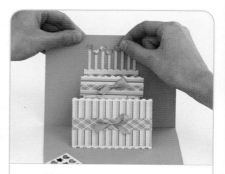

5 Stick the strips onto the tiers using double-sided sticky tape, then stick the tiers to the pop-ups, checking to make sure that the card can still be folded. Decorate the candles and surrounding card with stickers.

6 Score the second piece of card across the centre to make a single-fold card the same size as the first. Apply glue, avoiding the pop-ups, then stick the two cards together to form a neat outer layer.

Jewellery

Beading TECHNIQUES

A few basic techniques are all you need to assemble handcrafted jewellery. Keep pairs of jewellery wire cutters, snipe-nose pliers, and round-nose pliers to hand – they will help you achieve a neat finish to your jewellery. Although initially fiddly to handle, professional-looking wire loops can be made and jewellery findings attached quickly and efficiently with a little bit of practice.

Making a single loop

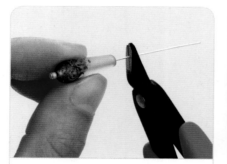
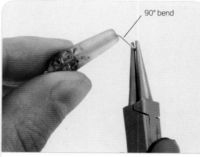

1 Slip a bead onto a headpin or ballpin, slipping a seed bead on first if the hole in your bead is too big. Snip off the excess wire 8mm (⁵⁄₁₆in) above the bead with wire cutters.

2 Hold the end of the wire with a pair of round-nose pliers. Bend the wire away from you at a right angle on top of the bead.

3 Turn your wrist to curl the wire towards you, making a loop. Release the wire, then grab it again to continue rolling it into a loop resembling a closed circle. A dab of superglue on the join will give added security.

Making a wrapped loop

1 Slip a bead onto a headpin or ballpin. Snip off the excess wire with wire cutters, leaving 4cm (1½in) above the bead.

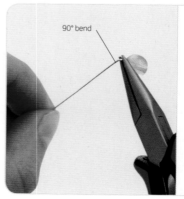

2 Hold the wire with a pair of snipe-nose pliers, resting the jaws on the bead. Use your fingers to bend the wire over the jaws at a right angle.

3 Using round-nose pliers, loop the wire around the jaw of the pliers so that the wire is at right angles to the wire emerging from the bead.

4 With the round-nose pliers through the loop to hold the piece steady, use your fingers to wrap the extending wire neatly around the wire emerging from the bead.

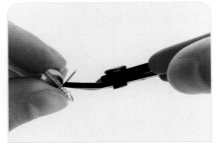

5 Snip off the excess wire close to the bead with wire cutters. Squeeze the snipped end close to the wrapped wire with snipe-nose pliers.

Attaching a bail

1 A bail has a claw on each side to hook onto a pendant or drop bead. Gently pull the claws of a bail open until the gap between them is large enough to slip a drop bead or pendant onto one claw. Slip the bead or pendant onto one claw.

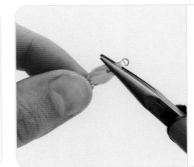

2 Squeeze the bail closed with snipe-nose pliers. Depending on the style of the bail, you may need to attach a jump ring to it (see below) to keep the component facing forwards.

Attaching a jump ring

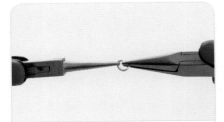

1 Jump rings join fastenings to necklaces and link components. Holding the jump ring between two pairs of pliers, gently pull one pair towards you until the ring opens wide enough to enable you to slip your jewellery component on.

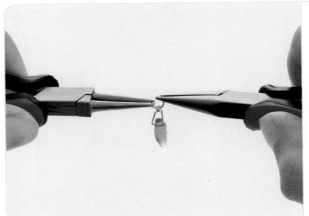

2 To close, hold the open ring between two pairs of pliers and push one pair towards the other, aligning the join. For extra security, dab the join with superglue or clear nail varnish, using a cocktail stick to deliver a tiny amount.

Threading beads

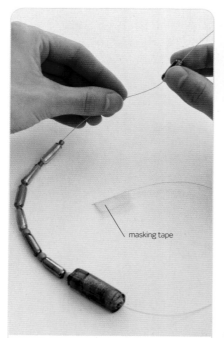

Wrap masking tape around one end of the beading wire or thread to stop beads slipping off. Thread on the beads, working outwards from the centre of your work. This allows you to add or remove beads either side of the centre to achieve the desired length.

masking tape

Attaching a crimp

1 A crimp is a tiny metal cylinder used to fix the ends of flexible beading wire. Slip one crimp then one jump ring onto the wire. Pull the end of the wire back through the crimp until the crimp sits 4mm (³⁄₁₆in) from the last bead and the jump ring 4mm (³⁄₁₆in) from the crimp.

2 Place the crimp in the inner notch of a pair of crimping pliers. Squeeze the pliers closed; the squashed crimp will be crescent-shaped. If you do not have crimping pliers, squeeze the crimp flat with snipe-nose pliers.

3 Position the crimp in the outer notch of the crimping pliers. Squeeze the pliers closed to round the shape of the crimp. Turn the crimp and repeat to improve its shape.

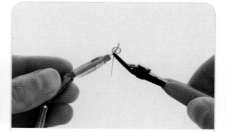

4 Snip off the excess wire as close as possible to the crimp with wire cutters. If making a necklace, repeat at the other end.

Fixing calottes

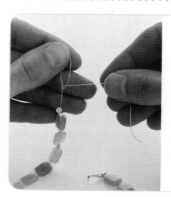

1 A calotte has two hinged cups with a loop attached. The knotted ends of strung beads are enclosed in the cups for a neat finish. Insert the thread at each end of a necklace through the hole in a calotte. Tie the thread in a large knot and cut off the excess thread. Glue the knot in one cup of the calotte with superglue.

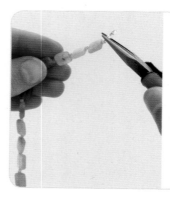

2 Squeeze the calotte cups closed with a pair of snipe-nose pliers. Slip the loop of the calotte onto a jump ring. Close the loop and repeat at the other end of the necklace, if this is what you're making.

Attaching a necklace fastening

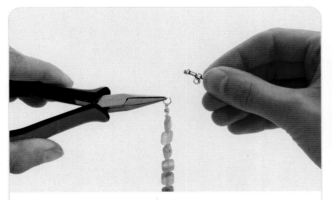

1 Use two pairs of pliers to open the jump ring at one end of the necklace. Slip the loop of one half of a necklace fastening onto the jump ring.

2 Close the jump ring using the two pairs of pliers. Apply a tiny dab of superglue or clear nail varnish to the jump ring join for extra security. Repeat at the other end of the necklace.

Attaching a tag end

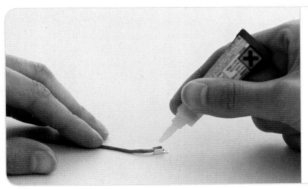

1 A tag end is a three-fold metal strip that secures the end of a thick threading material. Place the end of a cord, thong, or fine ribbon in the centre of a tag end. Glue in position with superglue. Allow the glue to dry.

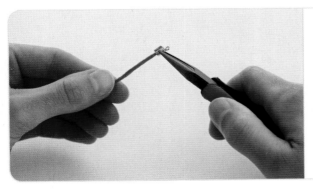

2 Fold one side of the tag end over with snipe-nose pliers, then the other side. Squeeze the tag end tightly closed with snipe-nose pliers. Fix a jump ring to the loop of the tag end.

Attaching an ear wire

Open the loop on an ear wire with round-nose pliers. Hook the loop of the earring component onto the loop of the ear wire. Close the loop with the pliers.

57

Beaded pearl necklace PROJECT

A pair of delicate heart-shaped beads anchors two strands of pearls at the front of this beautiful necklace featuring classic pearls in gentle colours. Pearl beads often have very tiny holes, so use the slimmest beading needles for this project. Remember to thread on the same number of pearls either side of the hearts.

YOU WILL NEED

- 160cm (64in) white bead-stringing thread
- embroidery scissors
- masking tape
- 2 short beading needles
- 2 x 1.2cm (½in) heart-shaped pearl beads
- 128 x 3mm (⅛in) natural round freshwater pearls
- 104 x 4mm (³⁄₁₆in) peach rice freshwater pearls
- 6 x 7mm (⁵⁄₁₆in) natural round pearls
- 2 gold calottes
- snipe-nose pliers
- 2 x 4mm (³⁄₁₆in) gold jump rings
- round-nose pliers
- gold toggle and ring necklace clasp

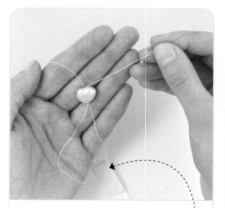

1 Cut two 80cm (32in) lengths of stringing thread. Join the threads with masking tape at their centre to stop the beads slipping off. As you'll be threading beads outwards from the centre, you'll be able to make changes to the beading sequence if you wish. Thread each thread onto a short beading needle. Thread both threads through the tip of a 1.2cm (½in) heart-shaped pearl bead.

2 Separate the threads and thread sixteen 3mm (⅛in) natural round pearls onto one thread and thirteen 4mm (³⁄₁₆in) peach rice pearls onto the other. Insert both threads through a 7mm (⁵⁄₁₆in) natural round pearl. Repeat this sequence twice. Separate the threads and thread sixteen 3mm (⅛in) natural round pearls onto one thread and thirteen 4mm (³⁄₁₆in) peach rice pearls onto the other.

3 Check the necklace length and how the pearls sit in a mirror. If necessary, add or remove pearls. Tape the beaded thread ends and remove the masking tape at the centre of the necklace. Thread on the second heart and pearls to match the first half of the necklace.

4 Insert both threads at each end of the necklace through a calotte, then slip the loop of each calotte onto a jump ring. Slip the loop of the toggle clasp through the jump ring and close. Repeat on the other side with the second half of the clasp.

Silver wirework TECHNIQUES

Fixing beads on twisted wires or binding an item with wire threaded with beads is a great technique for decorating plain jewellery and accessories such as a hair comb, headband, or bangle, or to make pretty pendants to hang on a necklace or ear wires. Use 0.4mm (28 gauge) or 0.6mm (24 gauge) wire and always start and finish the wire on top of your work, so it won't scratch skin or clothing.

Making a bunch of twisted stem beads

1 Thread one bead onto wire, leaving a tail 5.5cm (2¼in) longer than the intended length of the longest twisted stem. Hold the bead and twist the wires together to 5cm (2in) from the tail end.

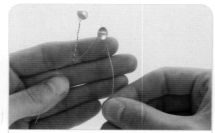

2 Bend the long end upwards and thread on another bead. With the bead just below the level of the first bead, twist the wires together under the bead until you reach the bottom of the first twisted stem.

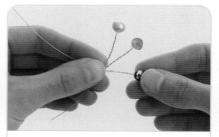

3 Again, bend the long end upwards. Thread on another bead and hold the bead just below the level of the second bead. Twist the wires together under the bead until you reach the bottom of the other twisted stems.

Binding with a bunch of twisted stem beads

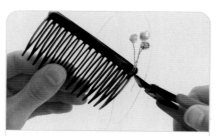

1 Bend the short tail of wire of the bunch around the item to be bound, finishing on the outward-facing surface. Snip off excess wire. Squeeze the end flat with snipe-nose pliers.

2 Bind the long tail of wire of the bunch under, and over the item a few times, pulling the wire taut as you work.

3 Continue binding the long tail around the item, adding beads if you wish. (See Steps 2 and 3 of **binding with wire and beads**, opposite.)

Binding with wire and beads

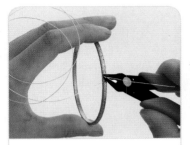  

1 Leaving a 5cm (2in) tail, bind wire around the item four times to secure it. Snip off the tail on the outer surface with wire cutters. Squeeze the end flat with snipe-nose pliers.

2 Thread on a bead and hold it against the outer surface. Again, bind the wire around the item, pulling the wire taut as you work. Continue adding beads and binding.

3 If you run out of wire, bind the wire four times around the item, finishing on the outer surface. Snip off excess wire. Squeeze the wire end flat against the surface with snipe-nose pliers, then bind a new length of wire over the end of the last wire. Continue adding beads and binding.

Finishing a continuous binding

When you reach the end, bind the wire four times around the wire at the start. Finish with the end on the outer surface. Snip off the excess. Squeeze the end flat against the surface with snipe-nose pliers.

Finishing a straight edge binding

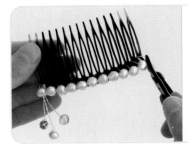

When you reach the end, bind the wire four times around the item, finishing with the end on the outer surface. Snip off the excess wire. Squeeze the end flat against the surface with snipe-nose pliers.

Making a pendant

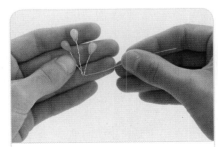  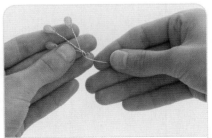

1 On a bunch of twisted stem beads, snip the short tail of wire level with the end of the twisted wires. Bend the other tail to a right angle.

2 Hold the tail with round-nose pliers close to the right angle. Roll the wire around the jaw of the pliers to make a loop. End with the tail at a right angle to the twisted wires.

3 Wrap the tail neatly around the twisted wires. Snip off the excess. Squeeze the end flat against the wrapped wire with snipe-nose pliers.

Sparkly tiara PROJECT

Make this pretty tiara to set off an outfit for a special occasion. Bunches of twisted stem beads stand proud of the headband and the sides of the band are bound with wire and beads. Bead shops sell plain tiaras ready to decorate, or use a narrow headband instead. A mixture of crystal, glass, semi-precious chips, and pearl beads have been used here, adding a touch of glamour.

YOU WILL NEED

- 8m (9yd) 0.4mm (28 gauge) silver-plated wire
- wire cutters
- selection of 3–6mm (⅛–¼in) crystal, glass, semi-precious chips, and pearl beads in assorted colours
- silver-plated tiara or 5mm (¼in) wide silver headband
- snipe-nose pliers

1 Snip a 1m (40in) length of wire. Follow **making a bunch of twisted stem beads** on p.60. Hold the bunch of twisted stems at the front edge of the centre of the tiara. Bind the short tail over and under the tiara. Finish on top of the tiara and snip off excess wire if necessary. Squeeze the end against the tiara with snipe-nose pliers.

2 Bind the long tail of the wire under and over the tiara four times. Thread on a bead to sit on top of the tiara. Bind the tiara four more times. Hold the tail upwards and thread on one bead 2cm (¾in) above the tiara. Bend the tail downwards. Twist the wires together until you reach the tiara. Repeat Steps 2 and 3 of **making a bunch of twisted stem beads** on p.60 using the same length of wire.

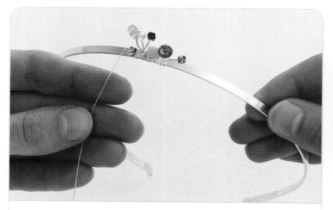

3 Bind the tiara four more times. Continue the sequence of adding beads, binding the tiara, and making twisted stem beads as you work outwards from the centre of the tiara.

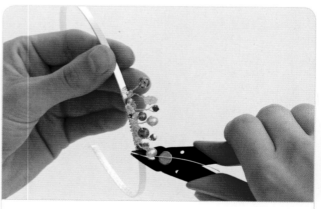

4 If you need to finish a length of wire and add a new length, follow Step 3 of **binding with wire and beads** on p.61. Continue making twisted stem beads and binding with beads for 8.5cm (3⅜in).

5 Snip a 150cm (60in) length of wire. Follow **binding with wire and beads** on p.61 to bind and bead the tiara, finishing 2cm (³⁄₄in) from the end of the tiara. To finish, follow **finishing a straight edge binding** on p.61. Decorate the second half of the tiara to match, starting by binding the short tail of the wire around the centre of the tiara.

Cold enamelling TECHNIQUES

No special equipment is needed for cold enamelling, yet with just the addition of a hardener, the enamels set rock hard with an attractive glossy sheen. There is a large range of enamel colours, which can be mixed to create new shades. Apply the enamels to metal jewellery bezels or blanks. Interesting effects can be achieved by swirling contrast-coloured enamels on a background colour or by applying glitter for extra sparkle.

Mixing colours

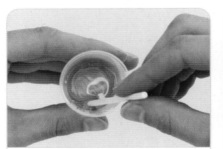

If you wish to mix your own colours, do so before adding hardener. Pour the enamel colours or drop them with a mixing stick or cocktail stick into a mixing cup. Mix the colours evenly with the stick.

Adding hardener

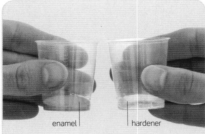

enamel   hardener

1 The enamel must be mixed accurately – two-parts of enamel colour to one-part of hardener. Pour two-parts of colour into a mixing cup. Pour one-part of hardener into another mixing cup.

2 Pour the hardener into the colour and mix. Leave to stand for 10 minutes to ensure there are no air bubbles. The mixture will remain workable for one hour. Prepare a second colour at the same time if wanted.

Cleaning metal

While the colour is standing, clean the bezel or blank with white spirit on a soft cloth. This degreases the surface.

Applying cold enamel

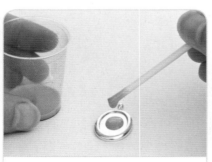

1 With the bezel or blank on a flat surface, apply the enamel to the recess with a mixing stick or cocktail stick.

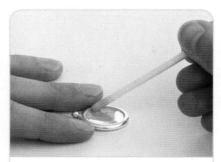

2 Distribute the enamel up to the outer edges, butting it against the frame of the bezel. Set aside for 24 hours.

Keeping a bezel level

plastic clay support

Often a bezel cannot be kept flat when applying the enamel and while it cures, such as on a ring for example. To keep the bezel level, support it on plastic clay.

Applying a second colour enamel

1 If a second prepared colour is applied immediately after its standing time on top of the first, it will spread on the surface. Apply the colour with a cocktail stick and swirl to distribute it.

2 Alternatively, leave the second colour to stand for a further 10 minutes, then apply it. You will not be able to spread it so much.

Applying enamel in relief

Apply a background colour and leave to dry for 24 hours. Use a cocktail stick to apply other colours in dots or swirls to the background colour. The other colours will stand proud of the surface. Set aside for 24 hours.

Applying glitter

1 Apply a background colour to a bezel and leave to dry for two hours. With the bezel on scrap paper, sprinkle fine glitter onto the background colour. Do not shake off the excess glitter. Set aside for 24 hours without touching.

2 Mix clear cold enamel with hardener (see **adding hardener**, opposite). Apply the clear enamel on top, completely covering the background colour and the glitter. Set aside for 24 hours.

Linked bracelet PROJECT

This charming bracelet is simple to make and is a great introductory project to cold enamelling. The enamelling is applied to bezels that have a loop at each side. These are linked together with figure-of-eight connectors. This bracelet has five bezels and is approximately 18cm (7in) in length. To shorten the bracelet, use fewer bezels; to lengthen it, add more bezels or link extra jump rings at one end.

YOU WILL NEED

- light blue and mint green cold enamel colours
- 3 mixing cups
- cold enamel hardener
- mixing sticks (optional)
- cocktail sticks
- 5 silver 3cm (1¼in) oval bezels with a link at each side
- white spirit
- soft cloth
- 6 silver figure-of-eight connectors
- snipe-nose pliers
- round-nose pliers
- 2 silver jump rings
- silver ring and bar fastening

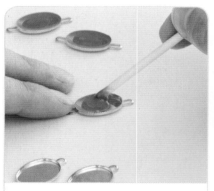

1 Prepare light blue and mint green cold enamel colours with hardener following **adding hardener** on p.64. While the colours stand, clean the bezels with white spirit on a soft cloth. Apply the light blue colour to the recesses of the bezels with a mixing stick or cocktail stick.

2 Set the bezels and mint green enamel aside for 10 minutes. Using a cocktail stick, swirl a circle of the mint green colour on the light blue background colour. Set aside to cure for 24 hours.

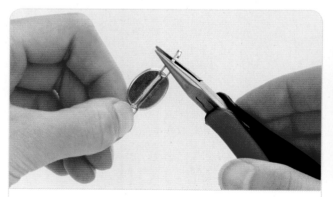

3 With the bezel face down, slip one loop of a figure-of-eight connector through one loop of the bezel. Squeeze the loop of the connector closed with snipe-nose pliers. Attach the other loop of the connector to another bezel. Repeat to link all the bezels.

4 Fix a figure-of-eight connector through the end loops of the first and last bezels and close with snipe-nose pliers. Slip a jump ring through the end loop of the first connector.

5 Slip the loop of the bar of the fastening onto the jump ring. Close the jump ring using two pairs of pliers. Repeat to fix a jump ring to the end loop of the last connector and the ring of the fastening to that jump ring.

Polymer clay TECHNIQUES

Polymer clay is a great modelling medium for making beads. Canework or millefiori beads – plain beads covered with thin decorative slices from canes of coloured clay – evoke the look of Venetian glass. To begin, knead the clay a little to produce a soft, pliable clay. Wash your hands regularly while you work to avoid mixing one colour into another.

Blending colours

Twist together logs of clay in different colours. Stretch and twist the clay, double it over, and repeat to create a marbled effect. You can use the clay at this stage or continue blending it to achieve an even colour.

Rolling a clay sheet

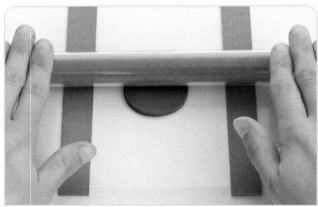

To roll clay to a specific thickness, place it on a non-stick sheet with a strip of card either side. Roll out using a non-stick roller. Vary the thickness of the card or layer the strips for thinner or thicker sheets of clay.

Making a jelly-roll cane

1 Roll two 1mm (¹⁄₁₆in) thick sheets of different coloured clays. Stack the sheets and cut to a 5cm (2in) square using a tissue blade. Flatten two opposite edges with a non-stick roller.

2 Starting at one flattened edge, roll the layers tightly and evenly. Roll the cane on a flat surface to smooth the join. Cut the ends of the roll level.

Making a flower cane

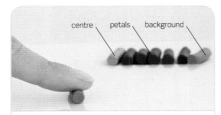

centre petals background

1 Roll eight 6mm (¼in) thick logs – one for the centre, five for the petals, and two for the background. Trim the logs to 3cm (1¼in).

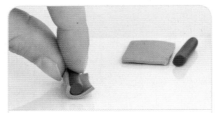

2 Roll a 1mm (¹⁄₁₆in) sheet of a fourth colour for the outer petals. Cut it into five 3 x 2cm (1¼ x ¾in) rectangles and wrap one around each of the petal logs. Roll to smooth the joins, then trim to 3cm (1¼in) long.

3 Arrange the petal logs around the centre log with the outer petals facing outwards. Cut the background logs lengthwise into quarters. Place a quarter between each petal log. Roll the cane a few times to smooth the circumference.

4 Roll a 2mm (¹⁄₁₆in) thick sheet of the background colour and wrap it around the flower. Roll the cane to smooth the join. See below to make pendants or continue to roll the cane to lengthen it. Cut the ends level.

Making plain and canework beads

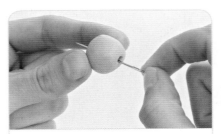

1 Roll a ball of clay and pierce a hole through the centre with a thick needle. Enlarge the hole with the needle and reshape. You can use scrap clay if the bead is to be covered in canework.

2 For canework beads, cut thin slices of jelly-roll cane and press them to the beads, butting the slices together. Fill gaps with tiny bits of matching clay. Roll the beads to smooth them, then re-pierce the hole.

Making pendants

Cut discs of canework 4mm (³⁄₁₆in) thick from a flower cane. Pierce a hole at the top with a thick needle. Bake the pendants flat on a baking sheet following the manufacturer's instructions. After baking, fix a bail through the hole (see p.55).

Baking beads

Thread beads onto a wooden skewer or thick wire for support while baking. Rest the skewer across an ovenproof bowl, then bake in a domestic oven following the manufacturer's instructions.

Polymer clay beads PROJECT

Make this pretty necklace to show off a set of canework beads. The beads are graduated in size and include spotted beads, which are quick and simple to make. Placing small, plain clay "spacer" beads between the larger beads emphasizes each decorative bead and helps them lay in a gentle curve. Of course, you could use glass or metal spacer beads for a change of texture.

YOU WILL NEED

- non-stick sheet
- light grey, dark blue, turquoise, and mid-blue clay, plus scraps of any colour
- 2 strips of 2mm (¹⁄₁₀in) thick card
- non-stick roller
- tissue blade
- thick needle
- wooden skewer or thick wire for baking
- 80cm (32in) flexible beading wire
- masking tape
- 2 silver crimps
- 2 silver jump rings
- crimping or snipe-nose pliers
- necklace fastening

1 Working on a non-stick sheet, blend a 3.5cm (1³⁄₈in) ball of light grey and a 1.5cm (⅝in) ball of dark blue clay to achieve a mid-grey clay. Blend a 2cm (¾in) ball each of light grey and turquoise clay to make a light turquoise clay.

2 Follow **making a flower cane** on p.69 to make a flower cane with a dark blue centre, light turquoise petals, light grey outer petals, and mid-blue background. Roll to 8mm (⁵⁄₁₆in) thick. Make a plain 2cm (¾in) bead using scrap clay and pierce a hole through the centre with a thick needle. Press flower cane slices in a row around the middle of the bead.

3 Follow **making a jelly-roll cane** on p.68 to make a jelly-roll cane with light grey clay inside and mid-blue clay outside. Cut a 4cm (1½in) length of the cane and roll to 6mm (¼in) thick. Roll the remaining cane to 8mm (⁵⁄₁₆in) thick. Cut slices from the smaller cane and press to the bead above and below the flowers. Roll the bead to smooth it, then re-pierce the hole.

4 From scrap clay, roll four 2cm (¾in) beads, four 1.5cm (⅝in) beads, and four 1.2cm (½in) beads. Apply flower cane slices to two beads of each size and 8mm (⁵⁄₁₆in) jelly-roll cane slices to the remaining beads.

5 To make the spotted beads, roll four 1.5cm (⅝in), four 1.2cm (½in), and four 1cm (⅜in) balls of mid-blue clay. Pierce holes through the beads with the needle. Roll a 1mm (¹⁄₁₆in) thick log of light grey clay, cut it into slices, and press to the mid-blue beads. Roll the beads to embed the spots then re-pierce the holes. Now make twenty-six 6mm (¼in) light grey spacer beads.

6 Follow **baking beads** on p.69, then thread the beads onto flexible beading wire. Graduate outwards in size from the centre, with the largest bead at the centre and a spacer bead between each decorated bead. Follow **attaching a crimp** on p.56 and **attaching a necklace fastening** on p.57 to complete the necklace.

Ceramics

Painting china TECHNIQUES

Working with ceramic paints is as close as you can get to colour glazing ceramics without having to invest in expensive equipment, such as a kiln, to fire and set the colour. Ceramic paints come in a vast selection of colours and are easy and safe to use. Paint onto your chosen piece of china and bake in the oven to heat-fix.

Priming the surface

Use a cloth dipped in white spirit to clean the ceramic surface so that it is grease-free and ready to work on. Leave to dry.

Sketching and transferring your design

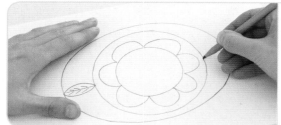

1 Sketch out your ideas on paper: it's a good idea to trace around the outline of your receptacle first to establish the frame within which your design must fit.

2 Once you are happy with your design, transfer it onto the ceramic. Since it is difficult to mark a glazed surface with pencil, transfer the design using a fine paintbrush and ceramic paints, then wash or wipe off any mistakes.

Experimenting with colour

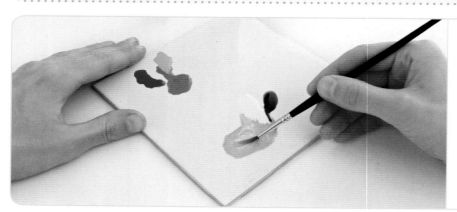

Use a plain white tile for mixing different colour combinations and experimenting with paint effects (think of the tile as an artist's palette). Adding white to a colour makes it look more solid and less opaque.

Achieving different effects with paintbrushes

Different brushes give different results: a soft-haired brush produces soft, delicate paint marks, whereas a coarse paintbrush gives a streaky effect. Use different width brushes to produce thinner or thicker lines.

Rinsing paintbrushes

Rinse paintbrushes in cold water as soon as possible after use.

Sponging

1 Pour a little ceramic paint into a shallow dish or onto a tile (rather than dip the sponge directly into the paint pot).

dry make-up sponge

2 Dip a dry make-up sponge into the paint and dab it onto the surface. You can build up stronger colour by leaving the paint to dry then sponging on another layer of colour. Rinse the sponge in cold water after use.

Achieving a sgraffito effect

This is a painting technique where the colour is scratched off to reveal the surface underneath. The term comes from the Italian word "sgraffire", meaning "to scratch". Drag a cocktail stick or the end of a wooden paintbrush handle into wet paint to achieve a scratched effect.

FIXING CERAMIC PAINTS

Once the paint is dry, place the painted ceramic in a cold oven and then set the oven to the recommended temperature. Bake for the stated time, turn off the heat, and leave to cool in the oven. Do not be tempted to remove the ceramic from the oven when it is still hot as the sudden change in temperature may make it crack.

Fruit bowl PROJECT

This simple but effective project transforms a plain white ceramic bowl into a novel fruit bowl that will brighten up any kitchen. The inspiration here is a watermelon, but you could just as easily use an apple, with the outer surface of the bowl painted red or green, the inside cream, and the pips painted in the bottom of the bowl.

YOU WILL NEED

- white ceramic bowl
- cloth
- white spirit
- coarse 1–2cm (⅝in) wide paintbrush
- ceramic paints in peridot green, coral red, and dark brown
- cocktail stick
- shallow dish
- make-up sponge
- ceramic tile
- fine paintbrush

1 Clean the entire surface of the bowl, inside and out, using a cloth dipped in white spirit. Leave to dry before painting the outside of the bowl.

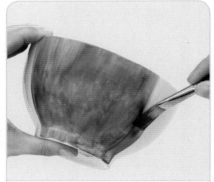

2 Using the coarse paintbrush, apply peridot green using swift, straight strokes. Start at the base of the bowl and work all the way to the rim. Try not to leave any gaps between strokes.

3 Work your way all around the bowl. Turn it upside down and, while the paint is still wet, brush it again with a dry brush to create texture. Work fast as the paint dries quickly but ensure the paint isn't too tacky as it may come off with the second brushing.

4 To create even more texture, add sgraffito work while the paint is still wet. Use a cocktail stick to scratch off lines of paint from the rim to the base of the bowl. Leave to dry for 24 hours.

5 Pour red paint into a dish and dip a dry make-up sponge in the colour. Dab the sponge on a tile to remove excess paint. Start in the centre of the bowl and work up the sides all the way to the rim to meet the green paint, dipping and dabbing the sponge as you go. Leave to dry for 15 minutes.

6 To paint the pips, dip a fine paintbrush in dark brown paint and paint pip-shaped dots inside the bowl. Don't overload the paintbrush or the paint will run. Leave to dry for 24 hours, then bake in the oven following the manufacturer's instructions. Leave to cool completely in the oven before removing.

Mosaics: the direct method

The direct method is a simple mosaic technique that is suitable for both flat and three-dimensional surfaces. One of its disadvantages, however, is that the adhesive is opaque and covers up the drawing as you work, so it's best to keep designs simple. The mosaic pieces are difficult to adjust once the adhesive has dried, so it pays to plan your piece out in advance.

Choosing your materials

Vitreous glass and unglazed ceramic are easy to cut, while marble and smalti have a traditional look and appeal. Glazed ceramic and broken china are usually coloured on one side only, so these work well with the direct method of application.

Cutting and shaping the tiles

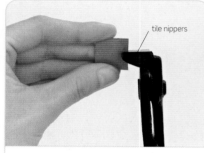

tile nippers

1 To achieve greater detail, quarter mosaic tiles before you begin. Place the tile nippers at the edge of the tile and squeeze gently while holding the tile with your other hand so that it does not fly away. Wear safety goggles to protect your eyes.

2 In order to create interesting patterns and representational designs, you can cut more defined shapes by placing the tile nippers at different angles and nibbling away at the edges of the tile.

Planning and transferring your design

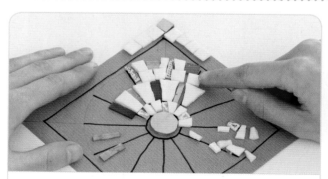

1 Draw your design on paper first. Lay out the cut tiles on your design, adjusting the colours and shapes until you are happy with the effect.

2 Copy or trace your design onto your chosen surface using a pencil or marker pen.

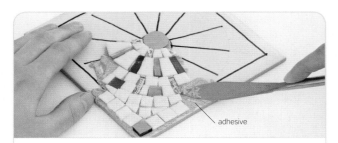

3 Mix cement-based adhesive with water to make a thick paste. Apply to the surface of the tile, using a plasterer's small tool or palette knife. Cover a small area at a time so that the adhesive does not skin over and the design is still visible.

adhesive

4 Carefully position the mosaic pieces in the adhesive bed. If you're not going to grout the tile, lay the pieces as close as possible, but if you are, leave even gaps between them. The size of gap can vary from 1 to 4mm ($\frac{1}{16}$ to $\frac{3}{16}$in) but it will look neater if the gaps are consistent.

Levelling the surface

If you're using mosaic pieces of slightly different thickness and want to achieve a flat final surface, add a little extra adhesive to the backs of the thinner pieces.

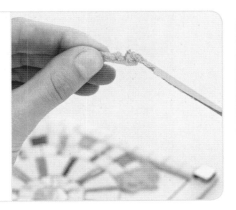

Grouting the piece

When the adhesive is dry, grout the piece. Mix the grout with water to form a thick paste and apply to the surface of the mosaic. You can use a grouting float to do this, but for small and 3D pieces it's easier to use your fingers protected by rubber gloves.

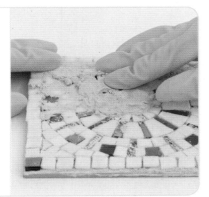

Removing excess grout

Clean off the excess grout with a damp sponge, turning the sponge over after every wipe so that you are always using a clean face. When the grout is almost dry, after about 20 minutes, clean off any surface residue with a dry cloth.

Flowerpots PROJECT

These flowerpots are embellished with a simple but effective mosaic decoration, made up of fragments of broken china and unglazed ceramic tiles. The pots used here are the plain rimless terracotta ones, but the technique works equally well on terracotta pots with rims (plastic pots are not rigid enough). The designs on the two pots echo each other: one has a blue flower design on a blue and white patterned background, while the background of the other is white and the flowers are patterned. This project uses the direct method.

YOU WILL NEED

- blue and white china plates
- towel
- hammer
- tile nippers
- 2 terracotta pots approx 15cm (6in) high
- 70:30 solution of washable PVA glue and water
- medium-size paintbrush
- pencil
- blue glass mosaic tiles
- cement-based adhesive
- plasterer's small tool or palette knife
- white grout
- sponge

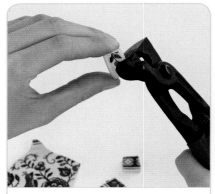

1 Wrap the china plates in a towel and smash them with a hammer. Cut the pieces into smaller, more regular shapes using tile nippers.

2 Seal the terracotta pot by painting it with the PVA solution and leave to dry.

3 Draw a simple design onto the pot in pencil and lay out the same motif on your work surface using the blue glass tiles. Cut these into strips to make the stem and into triangles for the flower and leaves.

adhesive

4 Apply cement-based adhesive to the pot's surface with a plasterer's small tool or palette knife, roughly following the design. Position the blue tile pieces on the adhesive, starting with the flower.

5 Fill in the background with pieces of broken plate. Choose pieces with a similar pattern to make a border around the rim. Apply adhesive to small areas at a time, turning the pot upside down to reach the base more easily. When the adhesive is dry, grout the piece and wipe away excess grout with a damp sponge.

Candles and soap

Candle-making TECHNIQUES

Once you have mastered these basic candle-making techniques, you'll be able to make a wide variety of candles, from coloured and fragranced candles to dipped and pillar candles. You may even want to experiment and make some novelty candles.

Choosing a mould

Candle moulds are receptacles into which wax is poured to create the shape of the candle. Professional moulds, made from materials including polycarbonate, plastic, latex, metal, and silicone can be purchased from specialist suppliers, but you can also use cake and chocolate-making moulds, as well as yoghurt pots and plastic soup containers.

Preparing your own mould

1 Wash out a container of your choice, such as a soup or yoghurt pot, and make a small hole in the bottom using a metal skewer. Secure a piece of wick, as explained in **securing the wick to the mould**, below.

2 If using a larger container, such as an ice-cream tub, you'll need more than one wick, so make two or three evenly spaced holes in the bottom of the container.

centre hole

Securing the wick to the mould

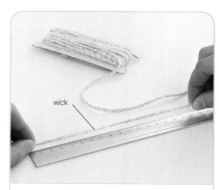

wick

1 Cut a piece of wick about 10cm (4in) longer than the depth of the mould and thread it through the hole in the base.

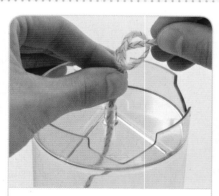

2 Tie a knot in the wick under the hole in the base to stop the wick from being pulled through.

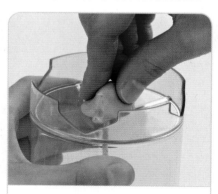

3 Seal the underside of the hole with Blu-tack or modelling clay. Make sure the wick is completely covered, with no gaps around it, otherwise the hot wax will leak out.

Making a wick holder

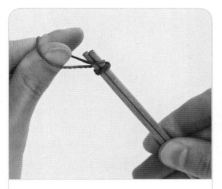

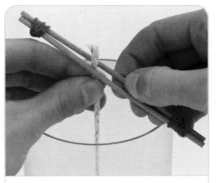

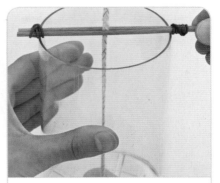

1 Wick holders keep the wick straight and taut in the mould. Secure the ends of two wooden skewers with elastic bands.

2 Insert the wick between the skewers and pull it gently so that it is fairly taut.

3 Rest the skewers on the rim of the mould, ensuring the wick is taut and centred in the mould.

Priming the wick

1 When making rolled candles (see p.88), the wick must be primed (coated in wax) first to ensure the candles light easily. To do this, melt a small amount of wax.

2 Submerge the entire wick in the melted wax: small bubbles will be released from the wick as it absorbs the wax.

wax-coated wick

3 After about a minute, or when there are no more bubbles, use a wicking pin or fork to remove the wick from the pan. Hold the wick over the pan so that any excess wax drips back into the pan.

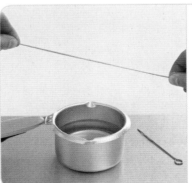

4 Allow the wick to dry for a few seconds, then, as it cools, pull it at both ends to straighten it.

Types of wax

beeswax

gel wax

soy wax

There are many types of wax. Most shop-bought candles use petroleum-based (paraffin) wax. However, there are some good alternatives, which are better for the environment and your home as they produce less soot. These are beeswax and soy wax, both of which are natural products and are cleaner burning. Soy wax comes in flakes, which are easy to measure out and melt. Soy wax is also soluble in water, making your pans and utensils easier to clean.

Measuring wax

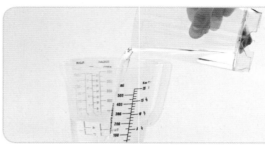

1 The easiest way to establish how much wax you need is to fill your mould with water after blocking the hole of the mould with Blu-tack. Pour the water into a measuring jug and make a note of the amount.

2 Convert the millilitres into grams (e.g. 100ml = 100g). Since melted wax weighs about 10% less than water, reduce the amount in grams by 10%: so for 100g of water you need 100g x 0.9 = 90g wax.

Grams of water	Grams of wax flakes
100	90
200	180
300	270
400	360
500	450
600	540
700	630
800	720
900	810
1000	900

Melting wax using a double-boiler

One-third fill the bottom part of a double-boiler with water and place the larger pan on top. Bring the water to simmering point, add the wax to the top saucepan, and melt, stirring occasionally with a metal spoon. As a rough guide, beeswax melts at 62°C (144°F) and soy wax melts at around 68°C (155°F). Refer to the manufacturer's guidelines for full instructions.

Melting wax using other appliances

Instead of a double-boiler, you can use a large saucepan partly filled with water, with a heatproof bowl on top. There are also purpose-made electric candle melters or, for small amounts of wax, you can use an electric chocolate fondue maker.

WARNING!

Never leave wax unattended when heating, and never let the temperature exceed 93°C (200°F).

Adding colour

1 The easiest way to colour candles is to use wax dye, available in liquid or flake form. The amount needed depends on the size of candle and the depth of colour required. As a rule of thumb, 1g (1/16oz) of dye will colour about 100g (3½oz) of wax, but do experiment first.

2 Once the wax flakes have fully melted, turn off the heat and add the dye. Stir it in thoroughly, particularly if you're using flakes rather than liquid. Bear in mind that the colour will look a lot paler once the wax sets.

3 If you're looking for a specific colour, test by dripping a small amount of dyed wax onto a plate and wait for it to set. If the colour is too pale add more dye; if it is too dark add more wax flakes.

Measuring fragrance oil

1 The amount of fragrance needed is usually specified by the supplier, but if using synthetic oil, you'll need between 5 and 10% of the weight of the wax. For essential oil, it's about 5%. You'll need to experiment and "burn test" your candles to make sure the fragrance "throw" (how well the fragrance is released into the room) is right.

2 Add the fragrance oil to the hot wax just before pouring. Stir it in thoroughly but carefully, and avoid adding air when stirring.

SAFETY FIRST

Place candles on a heat-resistant surface.

Burn candles in a well-ventilated room.

Extinguish candles when only 5mm (¼in) of wax remains.

Never leave burning candles unattended.

Keep candles away from draughts and flammable materials.

Keep candles out of reach of children and pets.

Store candles away from sunlight and direct heat.

Rolled beeswax candles PROJECT

Beeswax sheets are available in many colours, ranging from natural beeswax to all the colours of the rainbow. Before you start, make sure the wax is at room temperature so that it is pliable. If you need to warm the wax, use a hairdryer (taking care not to melt it) or place the wax close to a radiator for a few minutes.

YOU WILL NEED

- beeswax sheets
- cutting mat
- craft knife
- metal ruler
- primed square braided wick (see p.85)
- scissors

1 To make a straight rolled candle, place the beeswax sheet on the cutting mat and, using the craft knife and ruler, cut the sheet to 20 x 14cm (8 x 5½in).

2 Cut a 22cm (9in) length of primed wick. Place the wick 5mm (¼in) from the long edge of the wax sheet and gently fold the edge of the sheet over to cover the wick.

3 Start rolling the sheet, ensuring it is rolled evenly. Continue rolling to the end of the sheet. Press down the edge so that it doesn't unwind.

4 To make a slightly tapered candle, cut the sheet into a 20 x 20 x 28cm (8 x 8 x 11in) triangle, using the craft knife and ruler on the cutting mat.

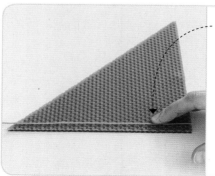

5 Place a 22cm (9in) length of primed wick 5mm (¼in) from one of the short edges and roll as in Steps 2 and 3. Press down the edge so that it doesn't unwind.

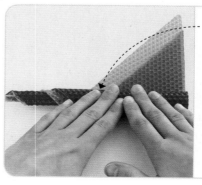

6 To make a double-layered tapered candle, cut two sheets into 20 x 20 x 28cm (8 x 8 x 11in) triangles, using the craft knife and ruler on the cutting mat. Place one triangle directly on top of the other, then follow Step 5.

Soap-making TECHNIQUES

The basic technique of soap-making involves melting a soap base and re-moulding it into bars or slabs filled with your own custom scents, colours, and additives. Once you have mastered these basics, you can branch out to create highly decorative soaps using techniques such as layering and embedding. The only limit is your imagination.

Preparing the soap base

1 Weigh out enough soap base to fill your moulds, allowing a little extra for wastage. Average-sized bars usually require 80 to 100g (3 to 3½oz) of soap. If you're not sure how much soap your mould requires, try cutting a slab to fit it.

2 Use a sharp knife to slice the soap into 2.5cm (1in) chunks. As a rule, the smaller and more regular the pieces, the more quickly and evenly the soap will melt.

Melting the soap base

1 To melt soap on the hob, place it in a heatproof bowl over a pan of simmering water until the soap becomes fully liquid. Stir occasionally but try to avoid generating air bubbles.

2 Small batches of soap can be melted in the microwave. Place the soap in a microwave-proof bowl and heat on full power for a series of 10-second bursts until the soap becomes fully liquid. Never overheat or boil the soap. It only needs to be warm enough to melt.

Colouring the soap

liquid dye

1 Liquid dyes and pigments should be added in tiny increments to the melted soap. Use the tip of a cocktail stick to add colour, one drop at a time.

2 If the colour isn't quite strong enough, add a little more dye and stir until it is fully incorporated into the melted soap.

powdered pigment

3 Add powdered pigment to a small batch of the melted soap and stir to dissolve it. Then incorporate this with the rest of the melted soap, little by little.

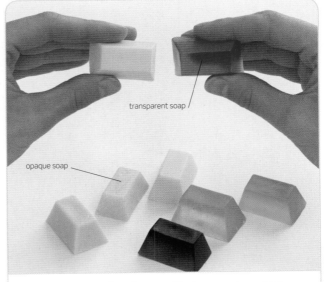

transparent soap

opaque soap

4 For intense, jewel-like colours, combine transparent soap base with liquid dyes or pigment. For flatter, paler shades, use opaque soap base with liquid or powdered colourants.

Scenting the soap

fragrance

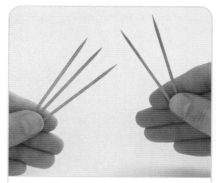

1 Add essential oils and fragrances to the soap just before moulding to minimize evaporation from heat. For small batches, add the oil drop by drop until the aroma is as desired.

2 For larger batches, measure out the fragrance into a beaker. Aim for 2 to 3% of the total weight of the soap, or 10 to 15ml (2 to 3tsp) per 500g (1lb 2oz) of soap.

3 When blending scents, experiment with top, middle, and base notes. Putting different combinations of dipped cocktail sticks in a ziplock bag is a good way to play with scent blends.

Enhancing soaps with natural ingredients

1 To add a luxurious, creamy texture to opaque soap, stir in a small portion of a solid moisturising oil such as shea butter while the soap is melting. Do not exceed 5g ($\frac{1}{5}$oz) per 100g ($3\frac{1}{2}$oz) of soap.

shea butter

melted soap

2 For an exfoliating soap, stir in a handful of finely ground oatmeal into the melted soap before moulding. Dried calendula or safflower petals can also be used to create a colourful, mottled texture.

3 For a decorative flourish, place slices of dried citrus fruit in the bottom of the mould and make them adhere by pouring a very thin layer of soap on top. After a minute or two, spritz with rubbing alcohol or surgical spirit then pour in the rest of the soap.

Moulding and storing soap

1 Once all the additives are in place, carefully pour the soap into the moulds. It is common for surface bubbles to appear after pouring; these can be dissolved by spritzing immediately with rubbing alcohol or surgical spirit. Leave to set.

2 After several hours, turn the mould upside down and flex each edge gently to release the soap. If the soap is stubborn, place it in the freezer for 15 minutes and try again. Once unmoulded, slabs can be sliced into bars using a knife or metal scraper.

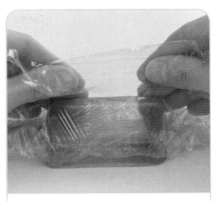

3 If the soap is not for immediate use, store it in clingfilm to prevent its high glycerine content from attracting humidity in the atmosphere and "sweating".

Layering and embedding

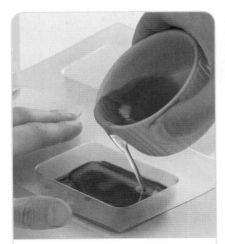

1 It is possible to create bars with multiple colours or scents by pouring in separate layers. Spritz the surface of the soap with rubbing alcohol or surgical spirit immediately after pouring, then leave to set. Spritz again before pouring the next layer.

2 Another popular technique is to embed small pieces of contrasting soap into the centre of the soap bars. These may be anything from simple, hand-cut shapes to decorative centrepieces, created with chocolate moulds or cookie cutters.

centrepiece

3 To create the finished bar, chill the centrepieces in the freezer for at least 30 minutes and then work as you would to layer the soap, placing the centrepieces in the middle layer of the soap. Spritz each layer with rubbing alcohol or surgical spirit before pouring the next.

Botanical slab PROJECT

Have you ever wandered around a craft market and admired the array of rough-cut, rustic-looking, natural soaps that are on offer? You too can produce your very own slab of soothing lavender soap that can be cut up into bars and shared with friends. The same approach can be used with a wide range of dried herbs, flower petals, and essential oils.

YOU WILL NEED

- 1 cup of dried lavender buds
- pestle and mortar or food processor
- 650g (1lb 7oz) goat's milk soap base, chopped into small pieces
- heatproof bowl
- saucepan
- metal spoon
- small measuring beaker
- 15ml (3tsp) lavender essential oil
- Tupperware container (approx 12.5 x 18cm/5 x 7in)
- metal scraper or knife

1 Divide the lavender buds into two equal portions. Finely grind one of the portions using a pestle and mortar or a food processor. Set aside.

2 Place the soap pieces in a heatproof bowl over a saucepan of simmering water and heat gently, stirring occasionally with a metal spoon until the soap has melted. Remove from the heat.

3 Add the lavender essential oil and the ground lavender and stir constantly for 1 to 2 minutes. This will help the lavender to remain evenly suspended within the soap. Allow the soap to cool slightly without setting.

4 Pour the mixture into the container. Before the soap starts to form a skin, immediately sprinkle over the unground lavender buds and press gently with your fingers to help them adhere to the surface.

5 Allow to set for several hours before unmoulding and slicing into smaller blocks using a metal scraper or knife.

Eco crafts

Basketry TECHNIQUES

Willow is a beautiful material to use in basketry, but you need to follow some simple guidelines for its preparation and handling. Once you've learned the basics, you can experiment with making different-sized baskets and work with more complicated weaves.

Selecting materials

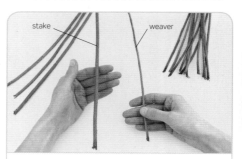

The stakes and weavers should be even in length and thickness. The stakes form the framework for the basket and the weavers weave around them. The stakes should be selected from a 5ft bundle of willow; the weavers from a 3ft bundle of willow. The thick end of the willow is called the butt; the thin end is called the tip.

Soaking and mellowing the willow

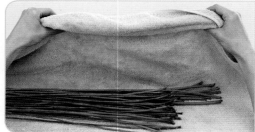

Willow is brittle when dry, so must be soaked by totally submerging it in cold water to make it pliable. After soaking, mellow the willow by wrapping it in a damp towel and leaving it overnight in a cool place to rest.

CALCULATING WILLOW SOAKING TIME

Buff willow has been boiled and stripped, so takes less time to soak than brown willow. Soak buff willow for 1 to 2 hours in cold water. Soak brown willow in cold water for one day per foot of willow (so 3ft willow will need to be soaked for three days). If you need to speed up the soaking time, use hot tap water and soak for a shorter time.

Making a cardboard former and framework

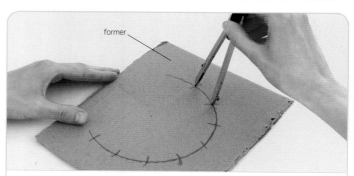

1 A former is used to hold the willow frame in the desired shape. Using a compass, draw an extended semicircle 15cm (6in) in diameter on a piece of cardboard, or draw around a plate of a similar size. Mark eight equally spaced points around the circumference. The points should be 3.5cm (1³⁄₈in) apart.

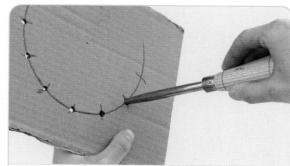

2 Make a hole through each point on the cardboard using a bodkin or skewer.

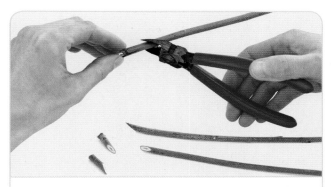

3 Before you feed the willow stakes through the holes to make the framework, cut a sharp angle across the butt end of the stakes using side cutters to help feed them through more easily.

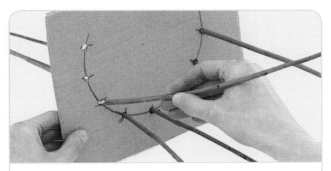

4 Push the first stake, butt end first, through the first hole until it is one-third of the way through. Push the next stake, butt end first, through the next hole from the other side of the cardboard until two-thirds of the stake is through. Continue pushing the stakes in alternately until they are all in place and the frame is completed. The ends should line up as a butt then tip, a butt then tip, and so on.

5 Tie one end of the stakes securely with string to hold them in place.

Basic weaving

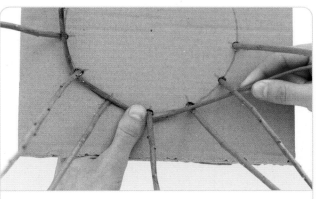

The weaving is worked by threading a weaver in front of one stake and behind the next. Each row of weaving should sit in the opposite place to the previous row. Use thicker weavers where the spaces between the stakes are big, and finer weavers as the spaces between the stakes become smaller.

Weaving around the edges

1 You can weave around the end stake by simply twisting the weaver around the stake and then weaving it back in the opposite direction.

2 To make a more secure edge, wrap the weaver tightly around the end stake twice before weaving it back in the opposite direction. This ensures the weaver holds the stakes tightly.

Joining weavers

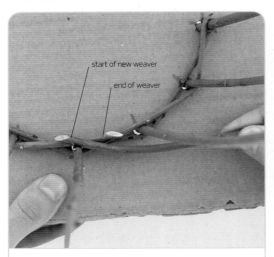

start of new weaver
end of weaver

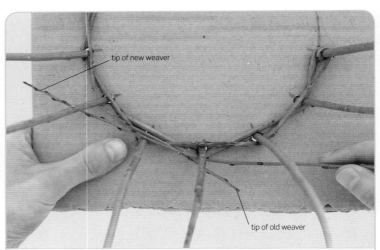

tip of new weaver
tip of old weaver

1 When you finish with a butt end, join in a new weaver by placing a new butt in the next space. Continue weaving with the new weaver. Leave the butt ends inside; they will be trimmed at a later stage.

2 When you finish with a tip, lay the tip of the new weaver over the old weaver so that they overlap and run together for a short distance. Continue weaving with the new weaver.

Finishing off

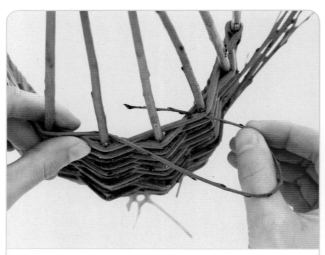

1 Always finish weaving a basket with a tip, tucking its end away under the previous row of weaving.

2 Trim away any ends using side cutters, making sure that each weaver rests on a stake. When the willow dries out it shrinks a little, so ensure you leave the weaver a little on the long side. You can trim it back further when it has completely dried.

Binding stakes

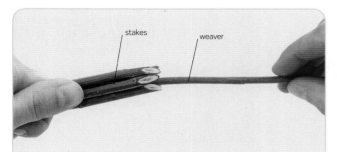

stakes   weaver

1 Binding is a method of tying the stakes of a basket together to make the framework secure. This is done after the weaving is complete. Trap the butt end of a weaver between the ends of the bunch of stakes, with the tip of the weaver pointing outwards.

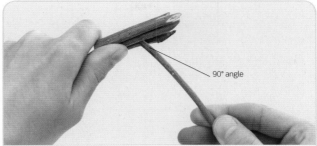

90° angle

2 Bend the weaver at a 90° angle, making sure that the butt end of the weaver is held firmly between the stakes.

3 Wrap the weaver around the bundle of stakes, keeping plenty of tension.

4 Continue wrapping the weaver until there are five rows of binding, each sitting alongside the next.

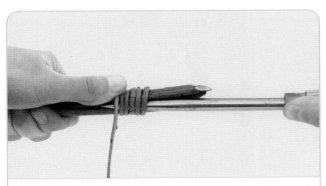

5 Holding the binding securely in place, use the bodkin to make a small space under the binding.

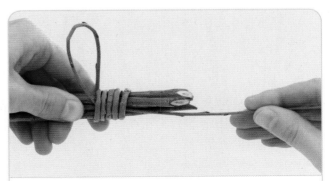

6 Remove the bodkin and feed the tip of the weaver underneath the rows of binding and back out in the direction it was originally pointing. Pull tightly to secure.

Willow fruit basket PROJECT

This quick and simple project uses brown willow to make a frame basket. The basket is woven around a cardboard former which holds the basket in shape while you concentrate on the weaving. Once you've mastered the basic weave you can enjoy watching the piece take shape. This basket makes a great fruit basket or looks good as a sculptural piece hung on a wall.

YOU WILL NEED

- stakes: 8 thick rods of 5ft brown willow
- weavers: 60 rods of 3ft brown willow
- towel
- side cutters
- cardboard former (see pp.98–9)
- compass
- string
- scissors
- ruler
- bodkin

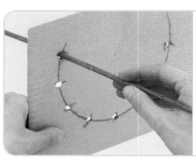

1 Soak and mellow the stakes and weavers, as shown on p.98. Push a stake through the first hole of the former, butt end first, until one-third of the stake is through. Push the butt end of the next stake through the next hole from the other side of the cardboard until two-thirds of it is through. Continue pushing the stakes in alternately until all eight are in place and the frame is completed. Tie the stakes together at one end with string.

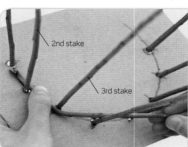

2nd stake

3rd stake

2 Begin weaving the untied side: place the butt of a weaver between the second and third stakes. Weave it in front of one stake, then behind the next. Wrap the weaver tightly around the last stake twice, then continue weaving in the opposite direction.

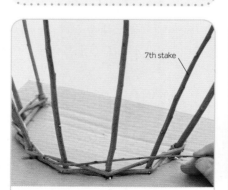

7th stake

3 Repeat until the weaver has travelled back and forth three times across the stakes, finishing on the opposite side to where it started. The tip of the weaver should sit on the outside of the seventh stake.

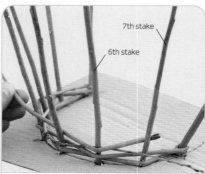

7th stake

6th stake

4 Place the butt of the next weaver between the seventh and sixth stakes and weave it across in the same way.

5 Continue weaving. Join in a new weaver at the opposite side of the basket to the last one. After weaving in six weavers, tie the ends of the stakes together with string to form a tapered end.

6 Continue weaving until there is about 15cm (6in) of weaving. Untie the ends of the stakes when they are too close to weave between.

7 Remove the cardboard former and tie string across the centre of the basket to hold the shape. Weave the second half of the basket in the same way as the first.

8 Bind the ends as shown in **binding stakes** on p.101. Trim any ends using the side cutters. Remove the string.

Pressed flower work TECHNIQUES

Follow a few basic principles and you'll find that pressed flower work can be most enjoyable. Flowers that press well and keep their colour include roses, buttercups, forget-me-nots, daisies, hydrangeas, and larkspur. Once you have more experience, you'll be able to press almost any plant material and achieve good results, though pressing fleshy flowers such as hyacinths and sedums may be more challenging.

Making a flower press

YOU WILL NEED

- 2 (5-ply) 15 x 20cm (6 x 8in) plywood boards
- 50 sheets newspaper cut into 15 x 20cm (6 x 8in) pieces
- 4 pieces 15 x 20cm (6 x 8in) smooth cardboard, 1.5mm (¹⁄₁₆in) thick
- 3 elastic bands, or 2 clamps, or 4 wing nuts and bolts

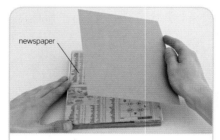

newspaper

1 To assemble the press, place one plywood board on the work surface and top with 10 sheets of newspaper. Place a thick piece of cardboard on top. Repeat the newspaper/cardboard layers until you have sufficient layers for the flowers you wish to press.

plywood board

2 Position the other plywood board on top to finish the sandwich. Hold the press together with elastic bands, clamps, or wing nuts and bolts. (If using bolts, you'll need to drill two holes either side of the plywood boards to accommodate the bolts.)

Pressing using other devices

paper tissue

Flowers may also be pressed between paper tissues in the pages of a heavy book. Place the book in a warm place to ensure the flowers will dry in one to two weeks. Other flower presses are available.

Choosing flowers and leaves

Only press perfect specimens and make sure you press more than you'll need as some petals and leaves will inevitably get damaged when you handle them.

CONSERVING FLOWERS AND LEAVES

To ensure flowers remain in excellent condition, pick them on a dry day and put into the press straight away.

Warmth and low humidity are essential when pressing flowers. These conditions help to remove the moisture content quickly from the plant material and keep the colours vibrant.

Pressing flowers and leaves

1 Place the flowers and leaves in the press between layers of paper tissues or other smooth, white absorbent paper, such as blotting paper. Don't use kitchen paper (you'll end up with dimpled petals) or newsprint (the ink will mark the petals and leaves). Put flowers of a similar thickness on the same page in the press. This will produce an even pressure when drying.

2 Small flowers may be pressed whole but larger ones, such as some roses, gerberas, and peonies must be taken apart and pressed petal by petal. Reassemble them when dry.

3 Large flowers, such as freesias, may be cut through the middle before pressing to produce two flowers from one.

4 As soon as the flowers are dry, remove them from the press using tweezers. If they are not being used straight away, store them flat, in a dry place, in clearly labelled envelopes.

Glueing flowers and leaves to card

dot of glue

Dip the tip of a cocktail stick into a rubber-based glue and dot onto the back of a flower or leaf before placing onto card. Use just enough glue to hold the flower in position.

Sealing the work

1 If you're framing your work, seal it under a sheet of glass or acrylic; if you're making jewellery, resin may be used.

2 For a greetings card or bookmark, use heat-seal film for best results. This film can be removed many times to replace straying flowers and when perfect, it is heated with an iron to seal the card. You can also use a normal self-adhesive film, but once applied it cannot be removed.

Greetings card PROJECT

Friends and family love receiving homemade gifts, and this pressed flower card depicting a vase of flowers will be no exception. The flowers, leaves, and stems are sealed in place so that they will not spoil when the card is taken out of the envelope.

YOU WILL NEED

- thick white card or blank greetings card measuring 30 x 40cm (12 x 16in)
- pressed tendrils (sweet pea, bryony, or passion flower)
- milk bottle top or jar lid to hold the glue
- rubber-based glue
- cocktail stick
- 3 or 4 different types of pressed flowers, such as larkspur, buttercups, potentilla (cinquefoil), and melilot (sweet clover)
- tweezers
- 2 different types of pressed leaves, such as alchemilla conjuncta (silver lady's mantle) and potentilla
- small scissors
- pressed grass stems
- self-adhesive or heat-seal film

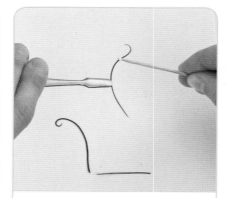

1 Fold the card in half then open it up. Work on the right-hand side of the card. Use the tendrils to create the sides and base of the vase. Apply a very small amount of glue on the back of each tendril using the tip of a cocktail stick and secure in place.

2 Arrange the flowers above the vase using tweezers so that the largest flower is level with the top of the vase. Arrange the flowers until you're happy with the design. Use some half flowers or buds to add interest, then glue the flowers onto the card.

3 Dot leaves in the gaps. If they are thin enough, tuck them under the flowers. Otherwise, cut the leaves and butt them up against the flowers.

4 Cut some pieces of grass to make stems of different lengths. Add the curly tendrils so that the straighter ends appear to go into the vase.

5 Use a piece of grass to create the water line and a few more to suggest a table. Scatter a few damaged or cut petals on the table to represent fallen petals.

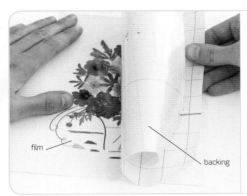

film

backing

6 Cut a piece of film slightly larger all round than the front of the card. Remove the backing and place the film over the flowers. If using self-adhesive film, ensure good contact is made around all the edges of the plant material.

7 If using heat-seal film, place a few layers of cotton fabric on top of the film and press using a warm iron for about 5 seconds: the small air holes will close when sufficient heat has been applied. Do not move the iron during this process. Trim the overlapping edge of the film.

Recycling TECHNIQUES

Natural materials are inexpensive (and often free) and can transform household accessories and ornaments into beautiful objets d'art. You can decorate a box with pine cones, make a pretty picture with shells and driftwood, or create a mosaic with small items such as cloves, seed heads, or even eggshell. Remember to prepare the natural materials carefully before use so that they don't smell or go mouldy over time.

Preparing natural materials

1 Wash out eggshells and boil in a pan of water for a few minutes to sterilize. When cool, peel away the membrane from inside the shell.

2 Soak non-porous items like shells and pebbles in a weak solution of bleach or boil in water to sterilize and kill any bacteria that may cause mould and odours.

3 Dry out pine cones and other porous objects by spreading them on baking parchment on a metal tray. Bake on a low heat for about 30 minutes.

Embossing recycled metal

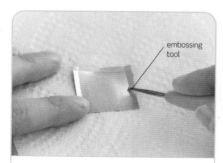

embossing tool

1 Lay a piece of aluminium cut from a drinks can on a pad of folded kitchen paper. Use a fine embossing tool to draw lines on the silver side of the metal. Rub the tip of the tool in a beeswax block to make it easier to draw with.

nylon-tipped embossing tool

2 To create a contrast in texture and also to keep the metal flat, turn the panel over and draw on the reverse side. For thicker lines, draw the motif freehand using a nylon-tipped embossing tool.

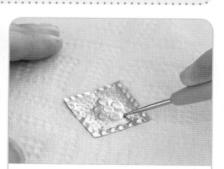

3 Turn the panel over to the right side and finish filling in texture. Use a fine or medium tip to add dots around the motif. You can also add dots or additional lines in a border for a more decorative effect.

Making eggshell mosaic

1 Slightly watered-down PVA glue has a longer drying time: use it to attach pieces of prepared eggshell. Position the pieces using a bamboo skewer, leaving even gaps between them. Attractive eggshells can be stuck face up; stick plain brown hens' eggs face down.

2 Paint the pieces of eggshell with acrylic or watercolour paint for solid colour, or water down the paint for a mottled effect. Leave to dry for 1 hour before grouting.

Grouting the eggshell mosaic

1 Fill the gaps between the pieces of eggshell with grout to create a smooth surface. Mix the grout with a little water to the consistency of thick cream (about 1 part water to 2¾ parts grout). Spoon the grout onto the surface of the mosaic.

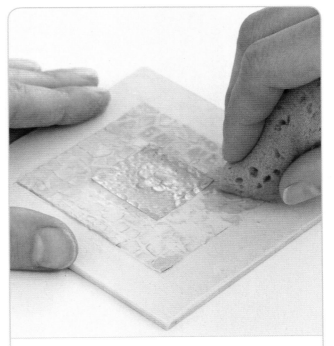

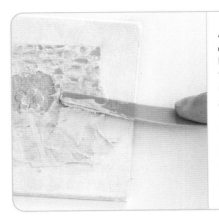

2 Using a flat-edged spatula or palette knife, gently smooth the grout over the mosaic. Work the grout into the crevices, allow to dry for a few minutes, then carefully remove as much of the excess grout as possible with the spatula.

3 Leave to dry for a few more minutes, then wipe clean with a barely damp sponge. Keep rinsing the sponge out in water as you go until the surface is clean but the crevices are still filled with grout. Leave to dry completely, then gently polish the surface with a soft cloth.

Eggshell picture frame PROJECT

This pretty mosaic frame looks so stunning that not many people will guess it's made from ordinary hens' eggs. You can use speckled eggs or even pale blue duck eggs if you can find them, but it's quite easy to colour plain eggshell with watercolour paint. This project is the perfect way to transform that charity shop find. Paint the frame white before you start to give it a neutral finish.

YOU WILL NEED

- pointed craft scissors
- aluminium drinks can
- scrap of paper
- pencil
- flat picture frame, painted white
- kitchen paper
- embossing tools
- strong PVA glue or epoxy resin
- fine and medium paintbrushes
- masking tape
- eggshells
- bamboo skewer
- black watercolour paint
- mosaic grout
- flat-edged spatula or palette knife
- sponge
- soft cloth
- matt acrylic varnish

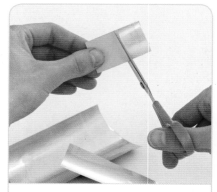

1 Using pointed craft scissors, carefully pierce an aluminium can and cut around the top and bottom. Cut along the length to create a rectangle. Make a paper template to fit the corners of your frame and use it to cut four squares from the aluminium rectangle.

2 Draw a border on the silver side of the metal squares. Refer to the template on p.126 to draw a heart shape and embellish it with dots. Draw some lines around the border on the reverse side both for decoration and to keep the metal flat.

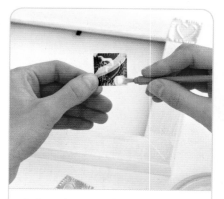

3 Use a strong PVA glue or epoxy resin to stick the aluminium squares onto the corners of the frame. Wrap masking tape across the corners to hold the squares in place until dry.

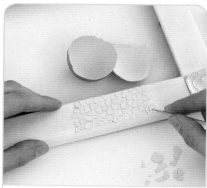

4 Prepare enough eggshells for the size of the frame, following **preparing natural materials** on p.108. Break the eggshells into small pieces and stick to the frame with PVA glue diluted with a little water.

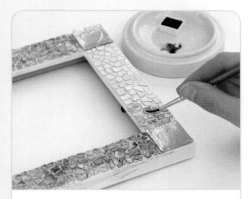

5 Once the glue has dried, mix black watercolour paint with water to make a wash and paint the pieces of eggshell to create a mottled effect. Leave to dry for about 1 hour.

6 Mix some mosaic grout with a little water to make a thick cream. Following the directions for **grouting** on p.109, apply the grout to the mosaic. Leave to dry completely, then buff with a soft cloth. Apply matt acrylic varnish over the mosaic to finish.

Tinwork TECHNIQUES

Tin plate is a versatile medium: it's strong, long lasting and can be decorated with a variety of finishes. Large, flat sheets of tin can be acquired by cutting open cooking oil cans and flattening out the metal. If you're painting metal, avoid water-based paints as they tend to flake off. If you prefer a natural finish, a coat of lacquer or Danish oil will protect the surface.

Choosing and cleaning the can

Choose a suitable can. Cans with a ring pull – and in particular sweetcorn cans – are ideal because they have a white lining that helps to reflect the light – perfect if you're **making lanterns** (see pp.114–15). Alternatively, you can use any tin can. Tear off the label and remove any blobs of glue with white spirit.

Packing the can

Before punching holes, you'll need to pack the can to prevent it from denting. Fill it with sand, press the sand down firmly with your fingers, then pour water on top until you can add no more. Place the can in the freezer overnight.

Punching holes in the can

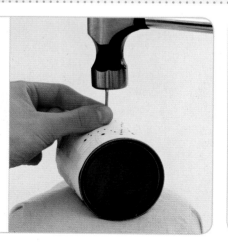

1 Masonry nails are hardened, so they are ideal for punching holes in tin cans. Place the can on a sandbag. To make large holes, punch with a small nail first, then punch in the same place with one or more larger nails to enlarge the hole.

2 If the nail sticks in a hole, use mole grips and a twisting action to remove it.

Making wire handles

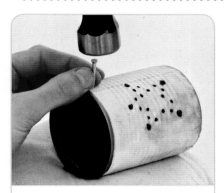

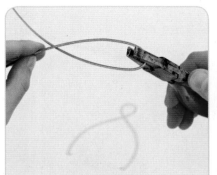

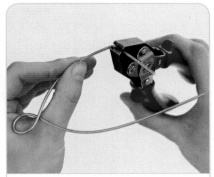

1 To add handles, punch a pair of holes opposite each other 1cm (³⁄₈in) below the top of the can. Once you've emptied the can (see below), cut a piece of coat hanger wire slightly longer than the final handle size.

2 Use ring-bending pliers to make a tight curve in the middle of the length of coat hanger wire. Use your hands to bend the ends into gentle downward curves, using the template on p.126 as a reference.

3 Bend the wire ends at right angles and trim these to about 3mm (¹⁄₈in) with a small pair of bolt cutters. Squeeze the handle to compress it slightly, then fit the ends into the holes in the can – the handle should hold in place by natural spring action.

Emptying the can

When you've finished punching holes, empty the can by placing it in a container and pouring on boiling water. Leave for 10 minutes to allow the ice to melt, then pour out the sand and water. Rinse and dry the can.

Painting the can

1 Fill the can with newspaper to protect the inside and lay sheets of newspaper over your work surface to protect it.

2 Spray the outside of the can evenly with the colour of your choice, then leave to dry for 24 hours. Alternatively, you can brush on an appropriate metal paint or apply a thin coat of oil-based paint.

Tin can lanterns PROJECT

It's remarkable what you can make with rubbish! Here's an attractive way to recycle tin cans into simple lanterns. This project uses small cans, but if you use larger ones, you might find glass jars that fit inside them to protect the candles from the wind. If you don't have any wire coat hangers, 2mm (¹⁄₁₀in) diameter galvanized fencing wire is a good substitute.

YOU WILL NEED

- tin cans
- cloth
- white spirit
- sand
- paper and pencil
- sticky tape
- fabric bag filled with sand
- masonry nails
- hammer
- small mole grips
- wire coat hangers
- small bolt cutters
- ring-bending pliers
- newspaper
- spray paint

1 Remove the label and any blobs of glue from the can. Pack the can with sand, top up with water, and freeze overnight.

2 Draw your design on a piece of paper to fit the size of the can or photocopy one of the templates on pp.125–26. Tape in place. If you're drawing your own design, ensure that the gap between holes is at least as large as the diameter of each hole.

3 Place the can on the sandbag. Punch holes in the can. Place the can in the freezer for about 30 minutes after each 10 minutes of work to ensure the can remains solid. If you're making several lanterns, work on them in rotation.

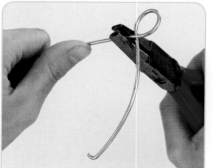

4 Once your design is complete, punch a pair of holes opposite each other 1cm (³⁄₈in) below the top of the can for fitting the handle. Remove the sand. Make a handle out of a 25cm (10in) length of wire, following **making wire handles** on p.113.

5 Fill the can with newspaper and spray-paint it evenly. Make sure you work in a well-ventilated area or outside. Once the can is dry, attach the handle.

Wirework TECHNIQUES

Wire comes in a myriad of types. If you are a beginner, copper wire is very good to work with as it is malleable. Many craft stores stock wire in a range of coloured finishes, and coat hanger wire is ideal when a strong structure is required. Household pliers can be used for wirework, but the serrated jaws can mark soft metals such as copper or aluminium.

Straightening a wire hanger

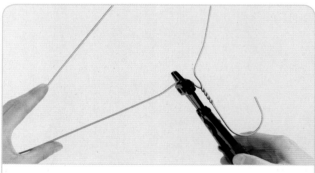

1 Cut the hanging loop and twisted section from the wire coat hanger using small bolt cutters.

2 Straighten the length you are left with – it may help to use mole grips to straighten the corners.

Straightening lengths of wire

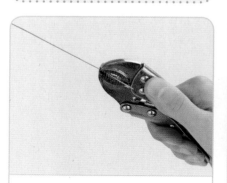

Pulling soft metal wire such as copper or aluminium to straighten it works well. Attach one end to a strong fixing point (a door handle for instance) and hold the other end in mole grips. Pull until the wire is straight.

Binding wire together

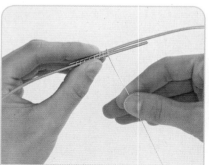

To bind two lengths of coat hanger wire together, overlap the ends by at least 5cm (2in) and wrap medium-gauge wire around the overlap until the ends are held firmly together.

Shaping wire

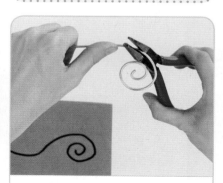

Gentle curves can be bent by hand, but for tighter curves in heavy-gauge wire, use a pair of ring-bending pliers – their smooth jaws do not mark the wire. If you're following a template, have it nearby for reference.

Twisting wires

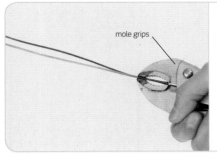

mole grips

1 If you need a long length of twisted wire, bend a length of wire in half, attach it to a strong fixing point (a door handle works well) and lock the two ends in a pair of mole grips.

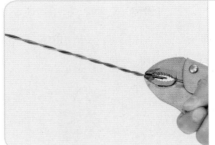

2 Pull the wire taut and turn the mole grips until you have an even twist along the whole length. Cut the wire to remove it from the fixing point.

Joining wires

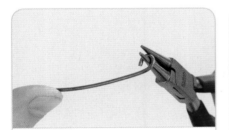

If you're working with wire and it breaks or runs out, attach another length by making a tiny loop in the end of each wire using round-nose pliers. Link the loops together, and press them closed with mole grips.

Wrapping wire

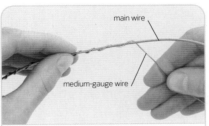

main wire

medium-gauge wire

Cut a length of medium-gauge wire one and a half times the length of the main wire. Curl the end of the medium wire around one end of the main wire, then wrap it around the main wire. Maintain tension so it is wrapped tightly and keep the spacing even.

Making a circular base

Bend a length of wire to form a circle. Overlap the ends by 4cm (1½in). Wrap a short length of medium-gauge wire around the overlap to hold the structure together.

Making a hanging jar

1 Cut a length of medium-gauge wire about 55cm (21½in) long and wrap it once around the jar, just below the lip. Twist the end around the wire to secure.

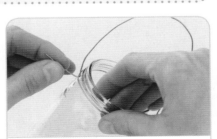

2 Pull the free end of the wire over to form a handle, then thread it under the loop around the jar. Twist the end to secure it onto the ring. Trim any excess wire.

Making an "S" hook

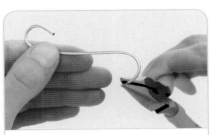

To make an S-shaped hook, curl one end of a 10cm (4in) piece of coat hanger wire using pliers to create a curve and the other end inwards to create a small loop.

Wire heart decoration PROJECT

This wire heart makes a perfect Mother's Day gift or a gift for a close friend. It's fashioned from a wire coat hanger and a handful of mother-of-pearl buttons. If you can't find any suitable buttons, use beads instead.

YOU WILL NEED

- wire coat hanger
- small bolt cutters
- mole grips
- ring-bending pliers
- fine 0.4mm silver-plated wire
- wire cutters
- superglue
- mother-of-pearl buttons

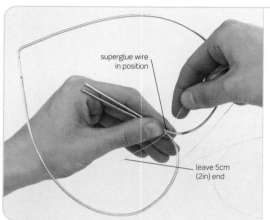

superglue wire in position

leave 5cm (2in) end

1 Cut the hanging loop off the hanger and straighten the hanger. Bend it following the template on p.127, using your hands and ring-bending pliers. Cut a 2.5m (8ft 2in) length of fine wire with wire cutters. At the top of the heart, where the curves meet, join the ends of the coat hanger wire with four of five turns of fine wire. Pull the wire tight, leaving a 5cm (2in) tail. Add a drop of superglue to fix the wire in position and leave to dry.

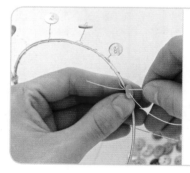

2 With the long end of the fine wire, make two loose turns along about 2cm (³⁄₄in) of the heart, then pull the end of the wire up through one hole in a button and back down through the other hole. Take care not to kink the wire as you pull it through.

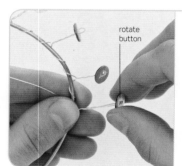

rotate button

3 Hold the button 1.5cm (⁵⁄₈in) from the heart and grip the two pieces of fine wire where they meet the heart. Rotate the button to twist the wire. Make two more turns of the fine wire around the heart, add another button, then repeat all the way round.

4 After the last button, make a couple of turns of the fine wire to return to the starting point. Take the wire through three buttons, adding a turn around the heart each time, then twist the 5cm (2in) tail of wire to finish off. Trim the twisted wire to 5mm (¹⁄₄in) and fix in place with a drop of superglue.

5 Cut a 30cm (12in) length of fine wire, bend it in half, and twist, following **twisting wires** on p.117. Form it into a loop. Tuck one end of the loop under the point where the first button was attached to the heart and bend the ends back on themselves. Trim the excess wire and cut off the ends of the wire hanger with small bolt cutters.

6 Fix the other end of the loop to the last button attached to the heart, as in Step 5. Add a button at the mid-point of the loop by threading a short length of thin wire through the button and fix in place by twisting the ends at the back. Trim the ends. Adjust the buttons so that they are arranged neatly around the heart. Add a dab of superglue to the back of each button to fix it in place.

Templates

120

Increase to required size on a photocopier

Throw (pp.26-27)

Throw (pp.26-27)

Bedspread (pp.22-23)

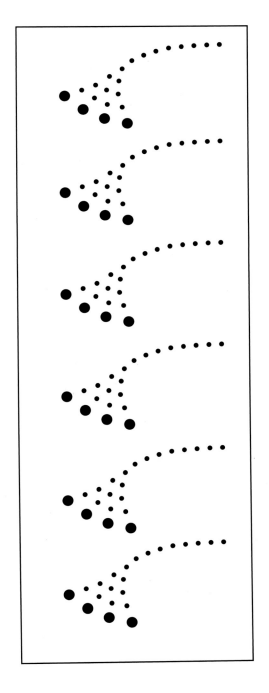

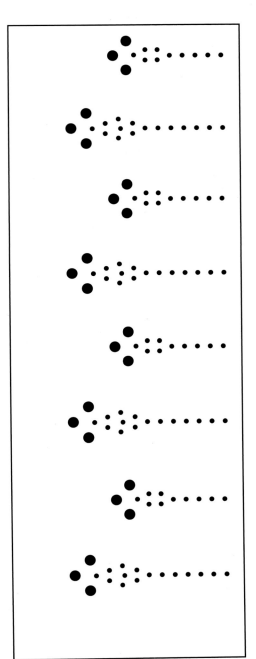

Tin can lanterns (pp.114-15)

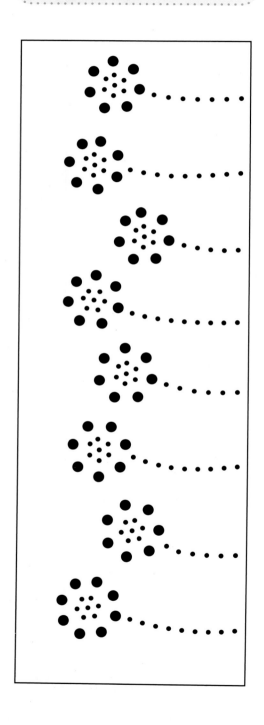

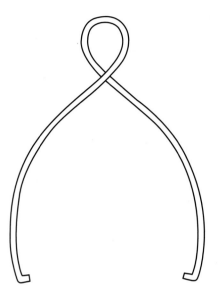

Picture frame (pp.110-11)

Enlarge/decrease to the required
size on a photocopier

126

Acknowledgments

Dorling Kindersley would like to thank Fiona Corbridge for her invaluable input in the early stages of development, Ira Sharma and Era Chawla for design assistance, Jane Ewart for photography art direction, Ruth Jenkinson for photography, Carly Churchill for hand-modelling and photographic assistance, Meryl Davies for photographic assistance, Hilary Mandleberg for sense-checking, Katie Hardwicke for proofreading, and Anna Bennett for indexing.

Craft 2012: Senior Editors Corinne Masciocchi, Hilary Mandleberg, Senior Art Editors Jane Ewart, Glenda Fisher; Project Art Editor Hannah Moore; Photographer Ruth Jenkinson; Photographic Assistant Carly Churchill; Managing Editor Penny Smith; Managing Art Editor Marianne Markham; DK INDIA Project Editor Charis Bhagianathan; Art Editor Prashant Kumar; Assistant Editor Swati Mittal; Managing Editor Glenda Fernandes; Managing Art Editor Navidita Thapa

The authors

Momtaz Begum-Hossain
www.thecraftcafe.co.uk / contact@momtazbh.co.uk
fabric marbling p.8, fabric painting p.12

Michael Ball
info@btnw.co.uk
tinwork p.112, wirework p.116

Jane Cameron
www.janecameron.co.uk / jane@janecameron.co.uk
batik p.16

Angie Corbet
www.vintagecraftstuff.co.uk / angie@vintagecraftstuff.co.uk
papermaking p.30

Sarah Ditchfield
www.candlebynight.co.uk / contact@candlebynight.co.uk
rolled candles p.88

Susan Flockhart
http://susiefhandmade.blogspot.com / susan@susanflockhart.com
botanical slab p.94

Tessa Hunkin
tessahunkin@blueyonder.co.uk
mosaics (direct) p.78

Fiona Goble
fkgoble@btinternet.com
appliqué p.24

Helen Johannessen
www.yoyoceramics.co.uk / helen@yoyoceramics.co.uk
painting china p.74

Susie Johns
www.susieatthecircus.typepad.com / susiejohns@colourful.co.uk
papier-mâché p.36, découpage p.40, quilling p.44, card-making p.48

Annemarie O'Sullivan
www.annemarieosullivan.co.uk
basketry p.98

Cheryl Owen
cherylowencrafts@aol.com
beading p.54, silver wirework p.60, cold enamelling p.64, polymer clay p.68

Denise Stirrup
www.realpressedflowers.co.uk / www.pressedflowerguild.org.uk
pressed flower work p.104

Dorothy Wood
www.dorothywood.co.uk / info@dorothywood.co.uk
patchwork p.20, recycling p.108